Turkey and the Dodecanese
– Cruising Pilot

Turkey and the Dodecanese – Cruising Pilot

Robin Petherbridge

ADLARD COLES LIMITED
8 Grafton Street, London W1

Adlard Coles Ltd
William Collins Sons & Co. Ltd
8 Grafton Street, London W1X 3LA

First published in Great Britain by
Adlard Coles Ltd 1985

Distributed in the United States of America
by Sheridan House, Inc.

British Library Cataloguing in Publication Data
Petherbridge, Robin
Turkey and the Dodecanese : cruising pilot.
1. Pilot guides—Dodecanese   2. Coasts—
Dodecanese   3. Pilot guides—Turkey   4. Coasts
—Turkey
I. Title
623.89′294996   VK867

ISBN 0–229–11716–3

Printed and bound in Great Britain
at the University Press, Cambridge

Contents

Complete List of Harbour and Anchorage Plans

Key to Symbols on Harbour Plans

General facilities

Symbol	Facility	Symbol	Facility
	Fuel	D	Dentist
	Water		Butcher
	Bottle gas	†	Church
	Ice		**Immigration officials**
£	Currency exchange	H	Health
	Chandler	P	Passport office
	Mechanic/Engineer		Customs
	Sailmaker		Harbour master/Port captain
	Post office		**Coastal features**
	Telephone office	+ (+)	Rocks or shallows
	Baker		Rocks which might be awash
	Laundry		Limit of 1m depth
	Showers		Yacht moorings stern-to
WC	Toilet		Anchorage/Harbour
	Hauling out		Beach
+	Doctor		Light

The cover photographs are reproduced by courtesy of the Turkish Tourism Information Office.

Part One

CRUISING THE AREA

CHAPTER 1

Weather and Navigation

WEATHER

Winds

Throughout most of the summer months, the daily winds, both in the Dodecanese islands and on the Turkish coast, conform to a reliably consistent pattern in direction, if not always in strength. From May to September the predominant wind in the SE Aegean is approximately NW, sometimes slightly more N as the season progresses. In the morning, winds are frequently only light and variable; then the NW wind generally comes up quite quickly within two hours after midday, and increases steadily to force four, five, or perhaps six, and then typically dies away between five and seven o'clock in the evening. At night there is often no wind at all, or only a very light breeze.

The predictability of this predominant daily pattern makes it particularly easy to plan a day's passage to take advantage of the wind, or the lack of it. However, it is much more difficult to predict – and even the local met. bureau has a poor record here – days when the wind either blows much stronger, or hardly at all, or comes from a different direction, or continues blowing strongly throughout the night.

For the amateur yachtsman there is certainly no easy way of telling when the pattern is going to break. Cloud is usually a sign of a change but not necessarily of stronger winds. Dry air tends to bring the stronger winds; and high humidity with night dew, lighter ones. If the NW wind continues blowing through the night, or gets up much earlier than midday, it can well reach over force six that afternoon. After a severe thunderstorm one can generally expect fair winds and fine weather for at least a couple of days, with excellent visibility. But these are only loose guidelines, based on my own observations over a number of years, and should certainly not be relied upon too heavily.

The other factor considerably affecting both the strength and the direction of the wind, is the land mass of islands, headlands and the shores of gulfs.

Because of the steepness and altitude of the landscape in this area, one finds that in the lee of the land, the wind is actually very much stronger and more gusty than a few miles off in open water. Furthermore, in many places the wind is deflected, sometimes by as much as 90°, to blow parallel to ridges of very high ground rather than straight over the top of them. To what extent the wind is re-routed in this way depends on the force with which it is blowing, and on the exact direction. A slight difference in wind strength or direction can result in a totally different path through the hills. Generally, the stronger the wind, the less it will be deflected from its overall prevailing direction.

But in any case, sailing close inshore with high ground to windward one should always proceed with caution, and keep a careful watch on the water for tell-tale signs of squalls and wind shifts.

The principal areas where the predominantly NW summer wind direction is considerably altered are as follows:

> Samos Strait: west or east
> Mandalya Gulf: west
> Gulf of Kos: west
> Gulf of Doris: west
> Rhodes channel: west or west-south-west
> Gulf of Fethiye: west-south-west or north-east
> South coast of Turkey: (see below)

From Kekova eastwards, the prevailing breeze generally follows the coast at reduced strength, as far as the Gulf of Antalya. Here, in the gulf, the afternoon breeze is usually only light to moderate, blowing up the gulf from the south, while the morning breeze is northerly, also only light to moderate.

In winter, from October to the following April, winds are much more variable, but unlike the summer, they tend to follow familiar pressure systems, and the local television and radio forecasters achieve a considerably greater degree of accuracy.

The worst conditions in winter are the severe gales that occur quite frequently from the south or south-east, but they can be from pretty well any direction from time to time. Although mainly confined to winter months, strong winds from the south will occur once or twice in May, and have been known in the early part of June. Similarly at the end of the season one has to be prepared for the occasional strong southerly blow in September, and certainly in October.

Weather Conditions

Although there can be periods in winter of a week or more of fine weather and light to moderate winds, few yachts sail in this season. Mostly the weather is cold, often windy, and wet, particularly around Marmaris and Rhodes which are notorious for winter rains.

From May to September one seldom sees cloud at all, except over very high ground, such as the Toros mountains around Kemer and Antalya, where there is some cloud most of the time.

Daytime temperatures of 60°–70° F (15°–21° C) in April increase steadily through May and June, and are usually in the 90s (32°–38° C) during July and August.

On the south coast of Turkey, from Kekova eastwards, average temperatures are 5° F or more higher than in the Aegean. In July and August the temperature here is frequently over 100° F, and if combined with high humidity can be quite uncomfortable, even in the shade, for many northern Europeans.

Temperatures in September and October are similar to those in June and May respectively. The range of temperatures in spring and autumn is much greater than in summer, and evenings and nights can be quite cold.

In late autumn, winter and spring, rainfall is considerable, but in summer there is seldom rain more than once a month.

Weather Forecasts

The only forecast in English on radio giving full information including wind strengths, is broadcast at 06.30 every day except Sunday by the Greek national radio station first programme. In the SE Aegean one can receive the transmission from Athens (728 KHz, 412 m), or Rhodes (1493 KHz, 200.9 m). East of Kaş even the signal from Rhodes becomes very weak, and reception is difficult.

The sea areas of interest covered by this book are referred to as Samos, Kos, Rhodes and Toros (the south coast of Turkey from Kaş to beyond Antalya).

PILOTAGE

Charts

British Admiralty charts are difficult to obtain locally. I have only seen them for sale in Rhodes, although they are of course available in Athens. Considerably cheaper, and quite satisfactory, are Greek charts, available in Rhodes and Samos, and excellent Turkish charts, available in Kuş

Adasi, Bodrum, and Marmaris. Translations of the Greek chart abbreviations are given in Appendix 2, page 209.

Tides, currents and sea conditions

Tidal rise and fall is nowhere more than 2 ft, and tidal streams are negligible.

Currents are variable according to conditions of wind, tide and barometric pressure, and within the area covered are never more than $1\frac{1}{2}$ knots. The more significant currents are marked on charts.

Sea conditions in the Aegean can often be troublesome in strong winds for a yacht making to windward. Seas are short and steep. Locals maintain that the most suitable hull for the area has a waterline length of greater than 60 ft to be able to bridge the waves, or less than 25 ft to ride up and down between them. Local craft seem to overcome the problem with the installation of generously oversized engines!

Like the wind, the run of the swell is greatly influenced by land masses, with a tendency to bend and follow coastlines. Also, whilst the swell is being driven by the wind it seems to be deflected less, whereas after the wind has died away in the evening, the swell that continues running for several hours can easily bend through more than 90° around headlands and into the mouths of bays; a point to bear in mind when selecting an anchorage.

Navigation aids and hazards

Beacons for radio direction finding are so few and far between as to be of very little use. The only one in the area operating continuously is Rhodes: (frequency 339 KHz, morse code RDS). Others, at the airports of Kos and Samos, and just outside Finike, are only intermittent and therefore of limited use as navigation aids.

Buoys and navigational marks are also thin on the ground, particularly to those yachtsmen used to sailing in NW Europe. Even isolated rocks awash or close beneath the surface are usually unmarked, so careful chart work and accurate navigation can be most important.

There are very few harbours or anchorages that can safely be entered at night without local knowledge, and a powerful spot lamp.

Navigating at night, or even in daylight, one needs to be wary of local boats fishing to avoid becoming caught in their tackle. The techniques that cause the greatest hazard to other craft involve either one boat laying out a net in a large circle, then closing it up and drawing the net aboard; or laying out the net in a square between four small boats at night, each boat being equipped with a powerful floodlight to attract the fish. In either case one should obviously keep well outside the area where the net is being laid.

One other hazard to night sailing in Turkey is that navigation light regulations would seem to be very loose, such that local boats, some quite large, have been seen showing both red and green lights viewed from more than 45° off the bow. This can be very confusing, and on seeing approaching navigation lights it is best to keep an open mind on the course of the approaching craft until its change of bearing becomes clear.

USING THE PLANS IN THIS BOOK

A key to the symbols used on the Harbour and Anchorage Plans is on page ix in the beginning of this book.

Unsuitable conditions for a mooring

At the start of each chapter is a quick reference list of the harbours and anchorages of which more detailed descriptions then follow. Included in this list is a column headed 'Open to' to indicate which wind directions will most likely make that particular harbour or anchorage unsuitable.

However, as already explained, the path of wind and swell is often entirely different close inshore to that prevailing at sea in open water. Therefore, to assist a yacht which is at sea in selecting a suitable mooring to head for, the wind directions given in the column are *prevailing* wind directions, that is, those winds, as they would be blowing out in open water, which would cause that harbour or anchorage to be subject to disturbing or dangerous swell. They won't therefore necessarily be the same directions as those given in the text, which only indicate in which direction a harbour or anchorage is actually, *physically*, open. (The 'fetch' is the distance travelled by the wind across open water. It is included here since it is a major factor governing the growth of waves, their height and length increasing proportionally with distance from the shore.)

The area plans at the start of each chapter showing the position of anchorages do not include details of navigation hazards, and should not be used for navigation.

The names of many towns, villages and bays in this area have changed under the occupation of different nations, some several times over the last few centuries. Wherever possible I have used the modern names in current usage, which, by and large, are those used on Greek and Turkish charts, and increasingly on up-to-date British charts.

MOORING

Mooring in harbours is most commonly the typical Mediterranean style either stern-to, or bow-to. This involves letting go the anchor as you approach a space on the quay (either forwards or astern) securing the bow or stern to the quay, then hauling up tight on the anchor. The most common problems with this method are either when a skipper takes insufficient care to drop his anchor between the anchors of boats to either side, crossing them over and causing all sorts of problems when someone tries to leave; or not setting the anchor properly or not hauling it in tight enough, such that if the wind comes up later, blowing onto the quay or beam on, the yacht veers off and puts excessive strain on the anchors of other craft beside it, sometimes causing a skittle reaction as anchors break out one by one to leeward under the strain.

The advantages of this style of mooring over mooring alongside are that it takes up much less quay space, it is much more difficult for vermin to get aboard from the quay, and for yachts with aft cockpits moored bows-to there is greater privacy from quayside onlookers.

In some anchorages it is often advisable to run out a stern line to the shore rather than anchor free, either because there is insufficient room to swing safely, or because the bottom falls away steeply from the shore. In the latter case it is preferable to have the cable lying up the slope from the anchor towards the shore rather than have the yacht swing round and pull the anchor down the slope.

One should bear in mind though, that held by the stern in this way if a strong wind comes up on the beam, the strain on the anchor is considerably greater than if the stern is let free and the yacht allowed to swing round head to wind.

Wherever possible I have tried to give a good indication of the nature of the sea-bed in an anchorage, so that one can select the most suitable anchor. Only where the sea-bed is likely to cause problems for almost any type of anchor, such as areas of shingle or stones, have I specifically mentioned that the holding is likely to be poor.

CHAPTER 2

Formalities and Fees

TURKISH FORMALITIES

Ports of Entry

Kuş Adasi	Marmaris
Güllük	Fethiye
Bodrum	Kaş
Datça	Antalya

Arrival in Turkey

Arriving in Turkish waters it is important to have the correct Turkish courtesy flag, of woven material, and with the star and crescent correctly shaped.

Documents required are passports (visas for some nationalities); the yacht's registration document (RYA international certificate for pleasure navigation is acceptable); written permission from the owner (signed and stamped by an official notary) if a private yacht is being used by anyone other than the owner; and three copies of a crew list (detailing the ship's name, registration and tonnage details, the names of all the people on board with nationalities, passport numbers and dates of birth) signed by the skipper. With all of these papers, the skipper must report to the immigration authorities in the following order:

(1) Health Office (Sihiye)
   Will issue a certificate of a healthy ship in exchange for one crew list and a very small stamp duty fee.
(2) Passport Office (Pasaport Merkezi)
   The passport stamp is normally valid for a stay of up to three months but can be extended (see below).
(3) Customs (Gumruk)
   A transit log is issued, valid for 12 months which becomes the ship's papers whilst cruising in Turkey. The fee for this is $10 (1984),

payable in local currency. Foreign currency, liquor, tobacco, firearms, diving equipment, and specified items of yacht equipment have to be declared and entered in the transit log. All equipment listed must be aboard when the yacht eventually leaves the country.

(4) Harbour Master's Office (Liman)

Makes a stamp on the transit log. In some places, particularly marinas, this may not require a further trip to another office as there may well be a representative of the harbour master in the office where the transit log is issued able to make this stamp.

Transiting in Turkey

One normally need only show the transit log if requested by a customs official. At Ports of Entry the log is often kept in the customs office for the duration of the yacht's stay in that harbour.

Leaving Turkey

For clearance out of Turkey, the skipper should take the crew's passports and the transit log to the immigration authorities in the following order: (1) Harbour Master, (2) Passport office, (3) Customs.

GREEK FORMALITIES

Greek ports of entry in the Dodecanese

Samos – Port Samos
Samos – Pythagorio
Kos – Kos town
Rhodes – Mandraki

Arrival in Greece

Documents required are the same as for Turkey. The skipper should proceed to the immigration authorities in the following order:

(1) Passport Office

The passport stamp is normally valid for three months, and is not easily renewable. A crew list is required.

(2) Customs

A transit log, valid for 12 months, will be issued, in exchange for two crew lists and approximately £4.00 (1984) in local currency.

(3) Port Captain

The transit log may be delivered to the Port Captain's office for you, or you may have to take it there yourself. The log then remains in his office until the yacht leaves the port of entry to begin cruising in Greek waters, when it must be collected, and a further crew list is required.

Transiting in Greece

It is only necessary to show the transit log whilst cruising in Greece if requested by an officer from the port captain's office, except at Ports of Entry, where even if only passing through in transit it is usual to deposit the transit log with the port captain whilst the yacht stays in that harbour. Any official who asks to see the transit log may also request a further copy of the crew list for his own records.

Leaving Greece

The skipper should proceed to the immigration offices, with the crew's passports, in the following order:

(1) Passport Office
   For clearance to leave the country. A crew list will be required.
(2) Port Captain
   To collect and cancel the transit log. One or two more crew lists will be requested.
(3) Customs
   To deposit all the clearance papers.

OFFICE HOURS

Both in Greece and Turkey the immigration authority offices do not open until at least 08.00 hrs, so to make an early start one should complete exit formalities on the evening of the previous day.

PASSPORT STAMP EXTENSION

In Greece, obtaining a resident's permit to allow you to stay in the country longer than three months is almost impossible for the crew of a cruising yacht.

In Turkey, an extension of stay is possible on application to the central passport office of a Port of Entry or a major city. To facilitate the granting of an extension of stay it is important to retain all receipts from foreign currency exchanged, as this clearly distinguishes the bona-fide tourist from anyone illegally trying to take up employment and residence. Penalties in Turkey for overstaying the three months allowed are high.

TRANSIT LOG EXTENSION

Although one may hear of cases of transit logs apparently being renewed or replaced when their twelve months are up, it is most unusual, and one should certainly never plan a cruise with the expectation that one's transit log will be extended. The penalties, not to mention the legal and bureaucratic complications, if a yacht is still in the country after its transit log has expired, can be very serious.

The only exception to this occurs when a yacht is laid up. The customs office must be notified, and the period whilst it is out of use will not then count towards the twelve months allowed.

CERTIFICATES OF COMPETENCE

It is not required in Turkey or Greece for the skipper or crew of a private foreign yacht to have any certificates of competence. It is sufficient to enter 'amateur' on the transit log.

Charterers skippering a boat themselves *are* required to have competency certificates.

OPERATING FOR CHARTER

Yacht charter is a very sensitive issue in both Greece and Turkey, and regulations are updated quite frequently. One should therefore always check the current situation with the authorities if planning to operate one's own boat for charter.

At the time of writing (1984), it is possible for charterers to join a foreign flag yacht in Greece or Turkey provided that it sails immediately out of the country.

It is possible for a foreign yacht to obtain a licence in Turkey to operate cruises entirely in Turkish waters by making a contract with a Turkish charter agent. But obtaining the licence may take many months, or even years.

For a foreign flag yacht to operate charters entirely in Greece is not possible.

A foreign flag charter yacht may, however, enter and cruise in either Greek or Turkish waters just as any other visiting foreign yacht, but the yacht must enter and leave the country with the same crew, so that charterers must embark and disembark elsewhere.

FEES AND DUES

In the Dodecanese, apart from the initial expense of the purchase of a transit log, one may occasionally be asked for a mooring fee in larger harbours, but the amounts are nominal.

In Turkey in the high season, most harbours will have someone collecting mooring fees (often on a peculiarly *ad hoc* basis) which are usually of the order of £2 or so. Marinas are of course more expensive.

There is also the rather disorganised collection of lighthouse fees, which seem to be imposed about as often as they are overlooked. If charged, this will likely be a fee of a few pounds, and will cover a certain stretch of coast, perhaps 50 to 100 miles.

CHANGING CREW

The procedure for changing crews in Turkey is simple, and is described in the notes on your transit log.

In Greece one should also be permitted freely to change crew, but one sometimes may experience some hold-up, and non-cooperation if a Greek official suspects you might be taking on passengers for illegal charter.

CONTROLS

Once in possession of a transit log, a yacht should be free to cruise at leisure in Greece or Turkey without hindrance, but both countries are sensitive to yachts that might have entered their waters without completing the proper entry formalities, and on no account should one attempt to do this.

Whilst cruising the area, only on two occasions have I been randomly checked by patrols. Both occasions were in Turkey. The first was by a large customs launch in the Mandalya Gulf simply checking that the yacht's entry papers were in order for cruising in Turkey, and the second, a rather unexpected visit in the early hours of the morning by a customs officer whilst moored in Kuş Adası marina. This turned out to be because he suspected that a Canadian crew member returning to the yacht after dark was Turkish.

But both incidents were really no more than slight over-exuberance by the officials concerned, and on the whole one is most unlikely to be disturbed by any such unwelcome interference.

CONSULS

A British Consul is near at hand in Rhodes, and in Izmir, as well as the major cities of Athens, Istanbul and Ankara.

CHAPTER 3

Local Conditions and Facilities

POLLUTION, WASTE AND SEWAGE

Evidence of the generally rather inefficient disposal of waste and sewage is unfortunately frequently seen in this part of the Mediterranean. In the open sea, although the water appears chemically clean and beautifully clear, one frequently comes across large quantities of plastic bags and other floating non-biodegradable refuse, some of which can even be hazardous to craft making passage under power.

Harbours in Turkey I found to be fairly clean. All charter boats operating in Turkey are required to have holding tanks. Visiting craft without holding tanks should not use their toilets in any harbour. The Turks are fairly good at providing public toilets ashore, but in some places where this is not the case one can often use toilet facilities in a cafe or restaurant.

In Greece, harbours are too often filthy. In some, raw sewage from the town is actually discharged into the harbour. Despite this, it is prohibited for yachts to use their toilets in harbour, and there are seldom any public toilets ashore. However all Greek cafes and tavernas are obliged by law to have toilets, and one can often use these whether one is a customer or not.

The spillage of fuel oils in harbours is also a serious matter, and fines are heavy.

YACHT EQUIPMENT

For cruising in this area of the Mediterranean there are several items of equipment, perhaps not normally carried by a yacht from NW Europe, which can make life appreciably easier, safer, and more comfortable. Those most useful that immediately come to mind are:

Sun awning – preferably with side curtains, and which ideally can be left

up while sailing, particularly in July and August on the south coast of
Turkey.

Swimming ladder – preferably permanently fixed to the transom.

Stern gangplank – for medium and larger yachts that would normally moor
stern-to rather than bows-to in harbour.

Kedge anchor – easily handled from the stern, for smaller yachts that would
normally moor bows-to in harbour.

Mooring lines – two lengths for mooring stern-to or bows-to preferably
each with a loop of chain at the end to reduce chafe where mooring
rings on the quay are sometimes rather poor. Also a strong line of 50–
100 m is needed for running out ashore in restricted anchorages. A
fairly large loop of chain at the end of this will also reduce chafe where
the line is taken to a rock.

Echo sounder – even though one can frequently see the bottom at 10 m or
more, harbours are often too murky to see anything. Also, in deep
anchorages where the bottom cannot be seen, an echo sounder or lead
line is the only way to tell if the anchor is about to be let go in 15 m or
50 m!

Hose – the longer the better, together with several short lengths of
different diameter that can be slipped over the end to adapt it to various
sizes of tap.

Refrigerator – ice is available in quite a few harbours, but collecting it soon
becomes a tedious chore, and a refrigerator is a very nice thing to have
for storage of dairy products, cold drinks and drinking water.

Headsail roller reefing – with the frequently changing winds experienced
while sailing inshore on these coasts, headsail roller reefing to enable
one quickly to reduce or increase sail area is a tremendous energy saver.

Searchlight – essential if one expects to be entering harbours or anchorages at night from time to time.

Electric fan – very handy to keep the air circulating down below.

SUPPLIES AND PROVISIONS

Fuel

There are no problems finding supplies of diesel on the Turkish
mainland, but in many Greek islands supplies are rather makeshift. In
only a very few places is there actually a diesel pump on the quay, and with
a smaller boat with limited range it will sometimes be necessary to collect
fuel by canister from a service station. Greek taxis are not permitted to
carry cans of fuel.

Petrol (gasoline) is hardly ever available from a pump on the quay.

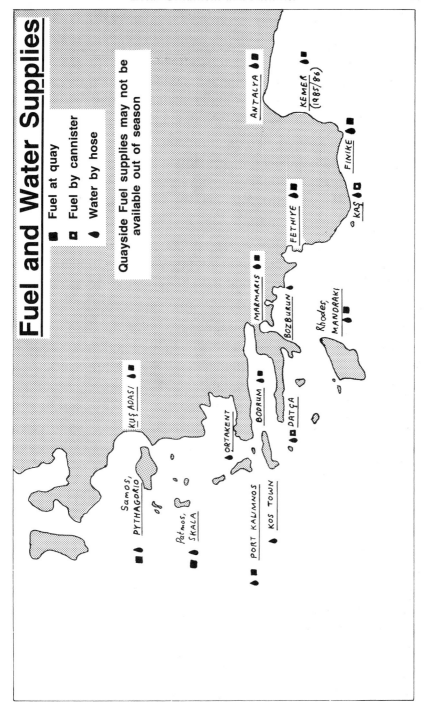

Fuel and Water Supplies

■ Fuel at quay
□ Fuel by cannister
♦ Water by hose

Quayside Fuel supplies may not be
available out of season

Water
On the Turkish mainland water is plentiful in most places throughout the year. Only Bodrum seems to have a serious problem with water in the summer.

In the Greek islands water is scarce in summer. It is a good idea always to take a can ashore with you when you go to a taverna for a meal, and they will normally agree to fill it for you.

Bottled gas
Only certain types of bottles can be exchanged in Greece (Camping gas being one type widely available) so that it may be necessary for a yacht equipped with foreign bottles to be adapted to use Greek bottles (deposit refundable).

In Turkey, the types of bottle available are even fewer, and conversion will almost certainly be necessary. I have only ever seen Camping gas available in Bodrum, Marmaris and Kaş.

BUSINESS HOURS

In Turkey the typical working day is from around 08.30 to 19.00 hours. Banks and offices are normally closed for an hour or two at lunch time. The post and telephone offices (PTT) are open six days a week, and some telephone offices are also open on Sunday.

Greek banks and shops open around 08.00, and close at lunchtime. Shops and some offices, but not usually banks, may open again in the evening from 17.00 until perhaps 20.00 hrs on Tuesdays and Thursdays, and sometimes on Fridays. Post offices are open five days a week, and only in the mornings. Telephone offices (OTE) are generally open six days a week, sometimes seven, and in major towns, 24 hours a day.

YACHT REPAIRS

Breakages and equipment failures can cause serious problems in Turkey and Greece due to the poor availability of spare parts. However, often a simple metal component can be made, or a broken one welded, and in fact both Turk and Greek alike are expert at finding an alternative to complete replacement of a broken or faulty part.

Parts can be sent from abroad but this necessarily takes time, and some duty will be payable.

Only the major boatyards at Kuş Adası and Rhodes are capable of doing work on modern yachts to a satisfactory standard. Even then, there will often be material supply problems, particularly of quality boatbuilding timbers such as teak and mahogany, and of marine grade plywood.

If requiring repair work to be carried out in Turkey, it is worthwhile employing the services of an agent who, for a reasonable commission will arrange for the work to be contracted out, and see it through to completion for you.

Sailmakers with good quality cloth and thread are few and far between, and it is worth carrying some sail cloth and thread on board. Where there is no sailmaker within easy reach to stitch or patch a sail, it can be worth seeking out a leather workshop where they will at least have a machine capable of sewing through several thicknesses of sailcloth, and can do a satisfactory temporary repair until a sailmaker can be found.

WINTERING

The safest place to winter afloat in the area is undoubtedly Kuş Adasi. Also, not far away is Cyprus, where many yachts winter afloat in safety in Larnaca. When the marina at Kemer is finished I am fairly certain that it too will prove to be a safe place to winter afloat.

Yachts also winter afloat in Bodrum and Rhodes, but neither is completely protected, and should only be considered if there is someone always on board or in attendance in case of bad weather.

Yachts can be hauled out and shored up for the winter in Kuş Adasi, Marmaris and Rhodes. It may even be possible to haul out small yachts at local fishermen's boatyards, but it is advisable to oversee closely such an operation if the yard is not used to handling keeled yachts.

HEALTH

Water
Neither in the Greek islands or Turkey is water drawn from a tap always completely safe for drinking. The installation of a filter in the outlet from a yacht's tank is the best way to avoid health problems. Alternatively, bottled drinking water can be purchased in most places.

Food
Fresh fruit and salad vegetables to be eaten raw must always be thoroughly washed in safe water, preferably with some sterilising tablets added, and stored well covered to protect them from flies.

Fresh meat should never be undercooked.

In more remote restaurants, particularly in Turkey, facilities for keeping meat are usually very poor, and locally caught fish, which will seldom be more than a day old, is a much safer choice.

Medical Facilities

In a yacht in this part of the Mediterranean one can often be some way from medical help in the event of an accident or sudden illness. It is therefore important to carry as comprehensive a medical kit as possible aboard, and to know how to use it.

I have indicated in the text in which places a doctor can be found, but if a patient requires hospitalisation, or more complicated treatment, they will have to be taken to a major town, or flown home.

Proper medical insurance is important for foreign visitors, as local hospital facilities are not up to the standards of northern Europe. If anything such as difficult or dangerous surgery were required, one would want to be sure one had sufficient insurance cover to be flown home immediately for treatment, without any question, rather than be treated locally.

Inoculations

At the time of writing (1984) it was recommended for visitors to this area to be inoculated against cholera, typhoid and tetanus, and also to take daily pills against malaria in Turkey. But always check with a doctor or vaccination centre for up-to-date information before travelling.

Vermin

Precautions, such as raising the stern gangplank at night, should always be taken to discourage rats, cockroaches and other vermin from getting aboard.

Care should also be taken when walking or sitting ashore in country areas, particularly in Turkey, as one frequently sees scorpions (painful, but not usually dangerous) and also occasionally snakes and poisonous spiders. If you are bitten or stung, the locals will almost invariably have previous personal experience, and will know the best immediate treatment.

TELECOMMUNICATIONS

In Greece the telephone office (OTE) is normally separate from the post office. There are coin operated phone boxes in the streets for local calls, but it is from the OTE office that one can conveniently make trunk or international calls. For almost all countries the system is automatic direct dialling, and one pays for the call at the end, according to units shown on a meter. Some OTE offices in larger towns also have telex facilities.

In Turkey, the post office and telephone office are combined under the name PTT. By comparison to Greece the Turkish system for international calls is very poor. One can either use an automatic direct dialling call box, in which case one has to feed the machine with previously purchased tokens at the rate of two or three a minute or one can book a call, connected by the operator, and pay at the end, but using this method it is often necessary to wait an hour or more to be connected. Larger Turkish PTT offices also provide telex facilities.

CHARTER FLIGHTS

If using commercial charter flights to get to or from Greece or Turkey, the restrictions that apply to these flights can seriously hamper cruising plans. Essentially, anyone wishing to leave the country on a charter flight must not have visited any other country during their stay, and if they have, may well not be allowed onto the plane. This obviously concerns anybody intending to cruise in this particular area, visiting Greece and Turkey, and unfortunately the airports of Kos and Rhodes seem to be those that enforce these regulations the most stringently.

TRANSPORT

For getting around in Greece, there are excellent, and very reasonably priced, inter-city coach services, domestic air services by Olympic Airways, and ferry services to all of the islands. Taxis are reasonably cheap, but visitors often complain of awkward experiences, particularly in larger towns and at airports, when taxi drivers are either very unhelpful, or try to overcharge them by not putting their meters to zero at the start of a journey.

In Turkey coach services are also extremely good, and extraordinarily cheap to a European visitor. The Turks also have some domestic air services operated by the national airline.

Taxis are even cheaper than in Greece, and the drivers usually a great deal more helpful and enthusiastic. Only in certain towns are Turkish taxis equipped with meters. If a taxi does not have a meter, the fare should be agreed before the journey commences.

For short journeys in Turkey there is also the Dolmuş. This is a large car or minibus that follows a set route, but not to a time-table. It only commences a journey when it is full. Passengers can usually be picked up or set down on request anywhere along the route.

One can cross from Greece to Turkey, and vice versa, either by plane or coach between principal cities, or by sea via the short crossings between Samos and Kuş Adasi; Kos and Bodrum; and Rhodes and Marmaris; or between Athens and Izmir.

Most of these services run regularly in summer, but only sporadically out of season, and in the case of the short sea crossings, according to demand.

CURRENCY/EXCHANGE

In Greek and Turkish banks, foreign currency in the form of traveller's cheques, notes, personal cheques guaranteed with a Eurocheque card, or well known credit cards such as American Express and Visa, are all usually accepted.

In Turkey one should always keep the receipts when changing money, as they can be used to change excess amounts of local currency back again before leaving the country.

In Greece such reconversion is not possible. Also, it should be noted that if unused Greek money is taken out of the country it should be in smaller denominations than 1000 Drachma notes, as these are not readily accepted by banks outside Greece, and are often exchanged for as little as half the going rate.

INFORMATION

Further information on any subject relating to a visit to Turkey or Greece can be obtained from the respective Tourist Board offices in London or other European capitals. The addresses in London are:

Turkish Tourism Information Office,
    First Floor, 170–173 Piccadilly,
    London W1
    Tel. 01–734–8681

Greek National Tourist Organisation,
    195–197 Regent Street,
    London W1
    Tel. 01–734–5997

Part Two

THE TURKISH COAST – MARMARIS TO KUŞ ADASI

CHAPTER 4

Marmaris to Gulf of Symi

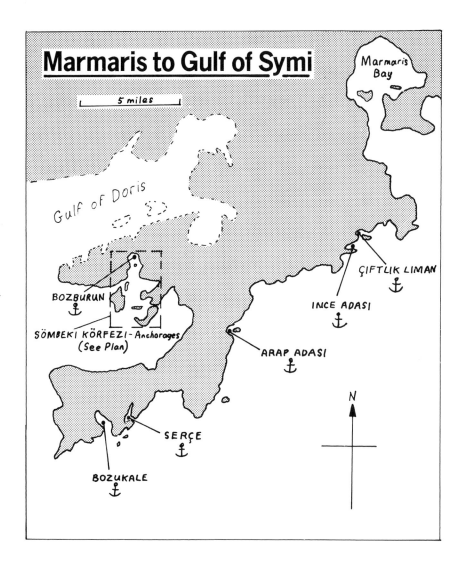

Marmaris to Gulf of Symi

Marmaris Bay

5 miles

Gulf of Doris

ÇIFTLIK LIMAN

INCE ADASI

BOZBURUN

SÖMBEKI KÖRFEZI – Anchorages
(See Plan)

ARAP ADASI

SERÇE

N

BOZUKALE

Harbours and anchorages

	Open to:	Comments:
Çiftlik Liman	S/SE	–
Ince Adasi	E	–
Arap Adasi	S/SE/E	–
Serçe Limani	–	Entrance difficult in strong S/SE winds
Bozukale (Aplotheka)	S	–
Gulf of Symi (Sömbeki Körfezi):		
Kizil Adasi	E/SE	Only for short fetch
Kiseli Adasi	E/SE/S	–
Bozburun Anchorages	E/SE	Only for short fetch
Bozburun (harbour)	SW	Only for short fetch

The anchorages described on this stretch of coast are all open to the SE to a greater or lesser extent. Since they are also all in the lee of high ground, in conditions of strong NW winds, they will be subject to gusty conditions. Of them all, Serçe provides the best all round protection.

ÇIFTLIK LIMAN   36°43′N 28°14′.5E   (No plan)

Here, in the bay behind the island Çiftlik Adasi, there are good anchoring depths on coarse sand off the beach. A chalet complex stands on the shore. Towards the SW end of the beach anchoring is not recommended as the bottom is very rocky.

From the W side of Çiftlik Adasi there is a power cable stretched across to the mainland shore, but it is high enough to clear the masts of all but possibly very large yachts.

INCE ADASI   36°42′.2N 28°13′.7E   (No plan)

Anchorage at the head of the inlet N of Ince Adasi in 5–6 m on a bottom of stones and sand. There is insufficient room to swing, so a stern line should be taken to a rock or tree on shore. Open to the E.

ARAP ADASI   36°39′N 28°08′.7E   (No plan)

Behind the islet of Arap Adasi anchor off the small stoney beach in 5–12 m depths on a bottom of sand and pebbles. There is ample room to swing. One can enter north or south of the islet, but the channel to the north is only 30 m wide, and has minimum depths of 4 m.

SERÇE LIMANI   36°34′.7N 28°03′E

Approaching from the E, the entrance to this almost land-locked natural habour lies beneath the highest of the peaks on the range of hills behind. Once inside, there are convenient anchoring depths at both the N and the

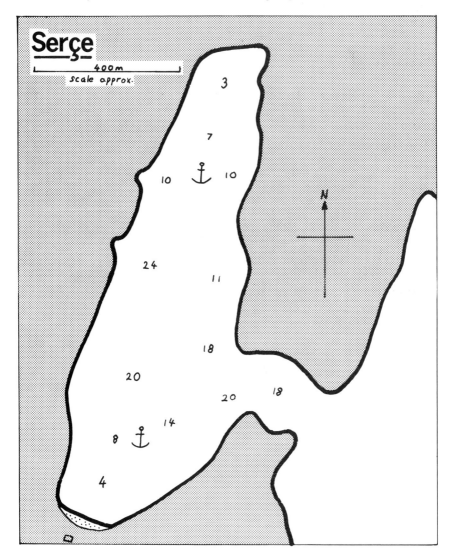

S end of the bay. To the N, the bottom is mud and weed and a stern line should be taken to a rock ashore as there is very little room to swing. At the S end, anchor on sand off the small summer café/restaurant, the only building in sight.

In strong SE winds, to enter the bay is difficult, if not impossible. A swell will enter. The better anchoring in such conditions is at the N end. Due to the lie of the hills to the W, a wind which is NW'ly out at sea will produce troublesome gusts, and may even appear to blow up the bay from the south.

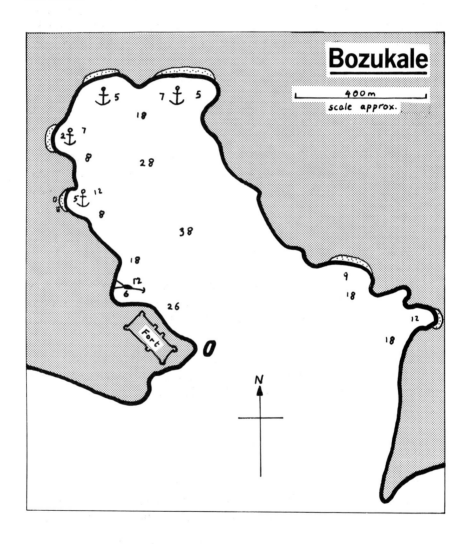

BOZUKALE (Aplotheka)   36°34′.2N 28°01′.1E

A quite large inlet 2½ miles E of Karaburun point, with a ruined fortress on the headland at the W side of the entrance. The only habitation is a couple of small stone shacks on the W shore, with a simple restaurant operating in summer.

The centre of the bay is deep, but there are convenient anchoring depths at the points shown on the plan on the W side, and at the head of the inlet to the north. At the anchorage marked immediately north of and just beneath the fortress, the bottom is steep-to, and it is advisable to take a stern line to a rock ashore. In the other anchorages it is possible to swing.

In NW winds the bay provides an excellent area of calm water for sailboarding. In SE winds, protection is limited.

SÖMBEKI KÖRFEZI (Gulf of Symi)

The recommended mooring spots in Sömbeki Körfezi, apart from the harbour at Bozburun, are small anchorages in the approach roads to the harbour in the enclosed area of water to the north of the island Kizil Adasi.

KIZIL ADASI   36°40′.2N 28°02′.3E

The eastern shore of the island has a rather steep rising sea-bed. Even at the preferred anchorage shown on the plan, it is advisable to take a stern line ashore to the west. Drop anchor in about 15 m on a bottom of sand and weed with stones. Open to E and SE.

Caution: The channel through shallow water to NE of the northern tip of Kizil Adasi is unmarked, and one should proceed with great caution. The maximum depth is about 2.5 m.

KISELI ADASI   36°40′.3N 28°02′.5E

Anchorage in the small bay on the east side of the island in 5–15 m on weed and sand. There is barely enough room for even a small yacht to swing so a stern line should be taken to a rock on shore. Open to SE.

Caution: The channel immediately NW of Kiseli Adasi is also very

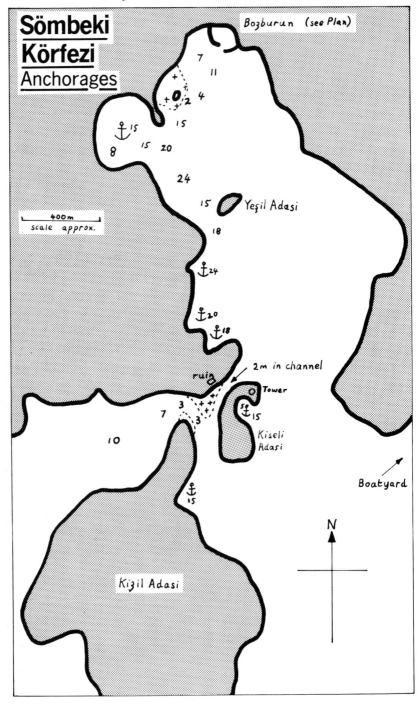

Sömbeki Körfezi Anchorages

Bozburun (see Plan)

7
11
O 2 4
15
15
8 15 20
24
15 Yeşil Adasi
18
⚓24
⚓20
⚓18

2m in channel
ruin
Tower
3 + +
7 5⚓15
3
10
Kiseli Adasi

Boatyard

⚓15

N

400m
scale approx.

Kizil Adasi

shallow, narrow and unmarked. The deeper water is found by staying closer to the shore of the island where there is about 2 m depth.

BOZBURUN – Anchorages
36°40′.7N 28°02′.4E   (No name)

Anchor in any of the three indentations in the shore to the west, between Kiseli Adasi and Yeşil Adasi. Depths between 10 m and 18 m, weed on sand, with a stern line ashore.

36°41′.3N 28°02′.1E   (No name)
Anchorage in the small bay ½ mile SW of Bozburun in 15–20 m. Weed on sand.

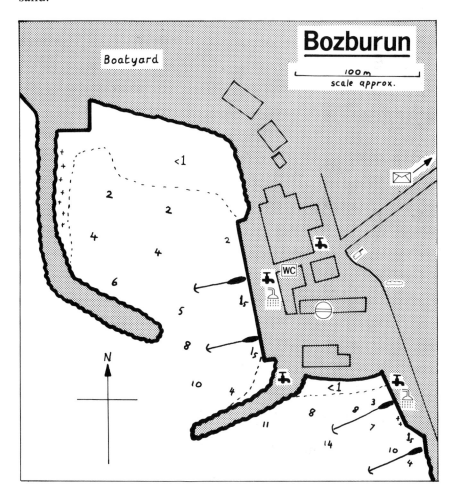

BOZBURUN   36°41'.5N 28°02'.7E

A pleasant and unspoilt little village with an excellent small harbour. The only visitors seem to be cruising yachts, and since the only approach by land is an unsurfaced road to Marmaris, some distance away, the place is unlikely to become developed.

Mooring
In the harbour one may have to moor bows-to rather than stern-to as the bottom rises close to the wall. Alternatively, go stern-to the quay to the E just outside the harbour wall. In strong S winds anchor in the harbour, and take a line to a boulder on the western breakwater, towards its extremity.

Facilities

There are a few restaurants open in the summer, and several cafes. Water points, and cold showers, are on the quay. The boatyard at the head of the harbour could slip a shallow draft boat. Buses run daily in the summer to Marmaris.

CHAPTER 5

Gulf of Doris (Hisarönü Körfezi)

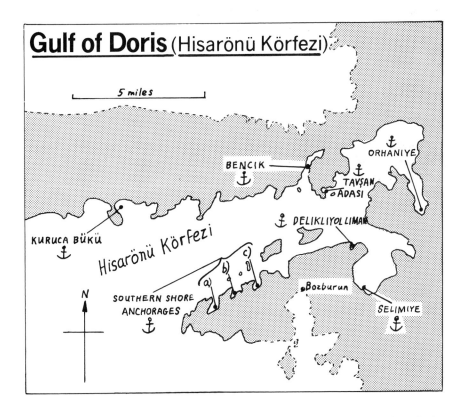

Caution: Sailing round Atabol Burun, the cape separating Sömbeki Körfezi from Hisarönü Körfezi, care should be taken to avoid Atabol Kayasi, an unmarked shoal 500 m WSW of the cape with rocks less than a metre under the surface. None of the rocks are visible.

Harbours and anchorages

	Open to:	Comments:
Hisarönü Körfezi,		
southern shore anchorages		
(a)	N	–
(b)	NE	–
(c)	N	–
Delikliyol Liman	NE	Only for short fetch
Selimiye	NE/N	For 2 mile fetch
Orhaniye	–	–
Tavşan Adasi	S/SE/E	For 2–3 mile fetch
Bencik Liman	–	–
Kuruca Bükü	S/SE/E	–

HISARÖNÜ KÖRFEZI – Southern shore anchorages

Four unnamed inlets on this shore offer reasonable shelter, and although open to the N, strong winds – in summer at least – are generally westerly blowing up the gulf, and should not make any of these bays unduly uncomfortable. All are isolated and uninhabited.

Anchorage (a)   36°41′.3N 27°58′.8E   (No plan)
One mile NW of the cape Atabol Burun is the first of the three inlets, which offers the best shelter of the three. Anchor towards the SW extremity of the bay, either side of the small rocky promontory in 5–10 m, on sand with weed patches. A stern line may be necessary as swinging room is limited. Partially open to N.

There is a shallow patch of rock SE-by-S from the entrance, in the centre of the bay, with a depth over it of 3.5 m.

Anchorage (b)   36°41′.7N 27°59′.4E   (No plan)
The centre one of the three inlets, and the most attractive, but with a very steep rising sea-bed towards its SW extremity offering an anchoring depth in excess of 20 m, and only a couple of large boulders to which to secure a stern line. Open N/NE.

Anchorage (c)   36°42′.1N 28°00′.6E   (No plan)
The eastern of the three inlets, immediately S of the SW tip of the island Koca Adasi, with again a rather steep-to bottom at its head, and 15–25 m depths, on weed and sand. A stern line could be taken to a tree. Open to N.

DELIKLIYOL LIMAN   36°43'.5N 28°05'.3E   (No plan)

1.3 miles E of the island Kameriye Adasi, is a small bay to the S as you enter Delikliyol Liman. It is isolated but attractive, with a fertile valley behind. The bottom is gently shelving, only 2 m depth 100 m from the beach at the head of the bay. Anchor in 3–8 m on sand and weed with room to swing. Open to NE.

SELIMIYE   36°42'.5N 28°05'.6E

The bay Selimiye Koyu has steep shelving sea-bed all around its shore, but on the SW side of the bay is a hamlet with a small quay where it is possible to moor bows-to. Depths are insufficient close up against the quay to moor stern-to. Even here the sea-bed rises quite steeply.

Facilities

One summer restaurant, and a couple of cafés.

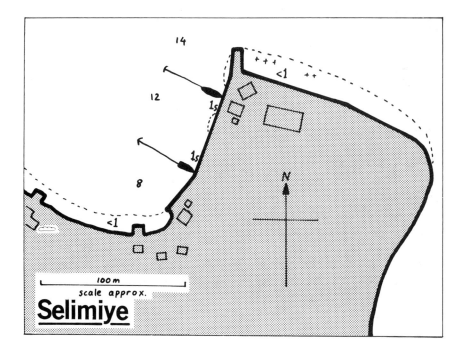

ORHANIYE   36°45'.5N 28°07'.6E

This long, narrow, very well protected inlet extends to the SSE from Hisarönü Limani which is the extreme NE portion of Hisarönü Körfezi. Unlike the dry barren hills of most of the gulf, here the shores are covered with pine woods, making it one of the more attractive anchorages in the area.

The water is a little murky, but only due to the muddy bottom. The inlet is reputed to be used by sand sharks for breeding in the spring, but these are apparently not dangerous.

Mooring

Anchor at the head of the creek off the small summer restaurant in 4–8 m on mud, or there is space for one or two boats bows-to the little stone jetty in front of the restaurant in 1.5 m next to the wreck of a concrete motor cruiser (1984). There are plans to refloat this, but to me such a scheme looked rather optimistic!

Alternatively, anchor either off the east shore opposite the little islet, where there is a conspicuous white restaurant (6–10 m on mud and weed); or in the narrow channel to the west of the islet, where depths are between 9 m and 12 m (weed on mud). If approaching this spot from the N, note that there is a bar running across from the islet to the west shore, which can only be crossed in the centre where the depth is 3 m.

Caution: The narrow mud spit projecting southwards towards the head of Orhaniye creek is awash, and although depths increase again to the east of it, the area with sufficient depths is too small to swing and should not be used for anchoring.

Facilities

Restaurants opposite the islet, and at the head of the creek, and also a rather incongruous small discotheque in the SE corner.

Cold showers and water by canister are available at the restaurant at the head of the inlet. Buses to Marmaris.

TAVŞAN ADASI   36°45'.9N 28°03'.2E   (No plan)

A remarkably isolated small anchorage, behind, and to the NE of the islet Tavşan Adasi, suitable in gentle conditions, with clear light blue water and shores of a most unusual lumpy brown rock.

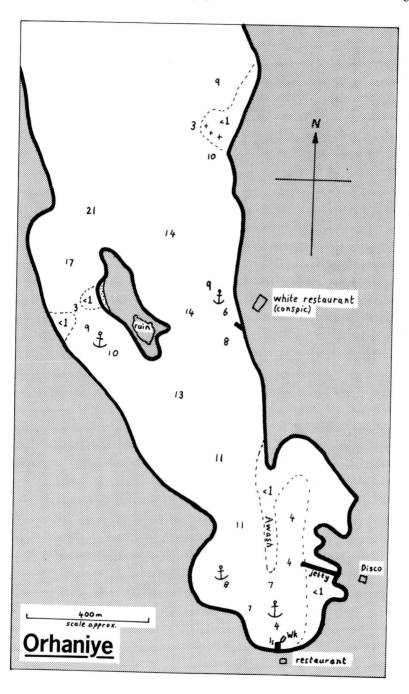

Orhaniye

Approach and mooring

One can enter to W or E of the islet, but care should be taken in the W channel as a rocky shoal stretches out westwards from the islet for some 100 m. One should therefore keep towards the mainland shore to the W.

Anchor in the extreme N portion of the bay, with the centre of the islet bearing 122°T. Depths are 5–15 m, and the bottom is sand and weed. There is room for a small yacht to swing, or one could find a rock on shore to run out a stern line.

Open to the SE quadrant.

BENCIK LIMAN   36°46'.5N 28°02'.4E

A very long narrow tree-lined creek on the N shore of Hisarönü Körfezi, popular with cruising yachts. It is uninhabited apart from a scientific installation on the E shore, on which it is prohibited to land. Shelter is exceptionally good.

Although sand sharks reputedly breed here in the spring, they are not supposed to be dangerous.

Approach and mooring

At the entrance to the creek is the lumpy brown islet Dişlice Adasi, and one can enter to E or W of this, but care should be taken to the W as at the narrow point between the island and the mainland shore there are rocky shoals off the shore and off the islet, so one must keep to the centre.

Inside the creek the bottom rises steeply to both sides, and a stern line to a tree is advisable in all the anchoring spots marked on the plan. Even towards the head of the inlet where depths are less, a stern line is advisable as there is barely room to swing. The area at the extreme head of the inlet is silted to less than 1 m. The bottom is sand and mud with some weed.

Caution: There is a submerged rock $\frac{2}{3}$ mile in an approximately SE direction from the islet Dişlice Adasi off the entrance to Bencik. The depth of water over this is only just over 2 m.

KURUCA BÜKÜ   36°45'.2N 27°53'.7E   (No plan)

A large and quite open bay, particularly to S and SE, but affording a useful protection from the W on this stretch of coast. As you enter the bay, a holiday apartment complex will be seen on the beach to the N. To the NW

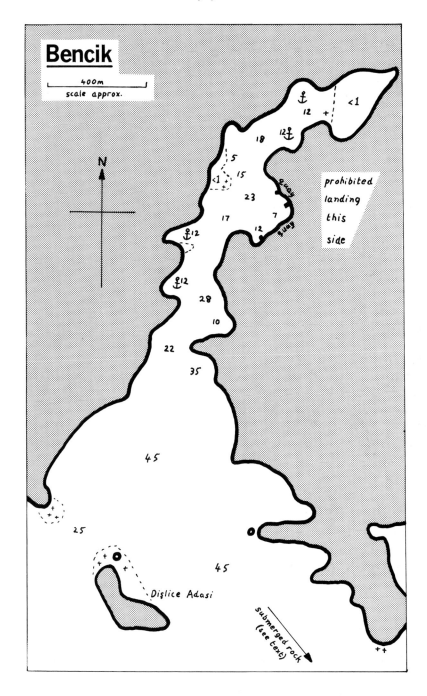

Bencik

400m
scale approx.

N

12

<1

18

12

5

15

<1

23

17

7

12

prohibited

landing

this

side

12

12

28

10

22

35

45

25

45

Dişlice Adasi

submerged rock
(see text)

is a conspicuous white disco-bar on another sandy beach, with woods behind, and a wooden jetty projecting out in front of it. Anchor anywhere in this area in 3–12 m on a gently shelving sandy bottom.

Cold showers are provided for patrons at the bar.

Another large bay immediately west, Çiftlik Liman, also has an extensive villa complex on the shore, to which the disco-bar belongs. However the shelter from the W in this bay is not as good, and anchoring is not recommended.

CHAPTER 6

Gulf of Doris to Gulf of Kos (Hisarönü Körfezi to Gökova Körfezi)

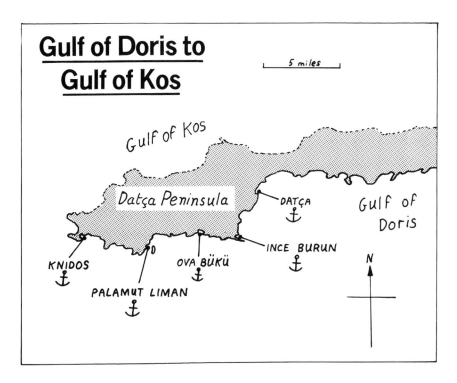

Gulf of Doris to Gulf of Kos

5 miles

Gulf of Kos

Datça Peninsula

DATÇA ⚓

Gulf of Doris

INCE BURUN ⚓

KNIDOS ⚓

OVA BÜKÜ ⚓

PALAMUT LIMAN ⚓

N

Harbours and anchorages

	Open to:	Comments:
Datça Iskelesi (harbour) Port of Entry	–	Some rebound swell in S/SE'ly winds
Ince Burun	SE/E/NE	–
Ova Bükü	SW/S/SE	–
Palamut Liman (harbour)	–	Difficult entrance in strong S/SE/E winds
Knidos	SE	Some protection from SE behind breakwater

DATÇA ISKELESI   36°43'.3N 27°41'.4E   Port of Entry

This pleasant and relatively unspoilt village has become increasingly popular with cruising yachts in recent years. Tourism ashore is also gathering pace with a number of pensions and a few hotels.

The village of Datça is 5 km inland, but the population seems to be shifting to the coast with the increasing business around the harbour.

Mooring

Bows-to in the harbour on the NW wall, or it may be deep enough in parts for smaller yachts to go stern-to. There is deep water to go stern-to the rock breakwater to the SE, but lines would have to be taken to rocks, and underwater rubble may prevent one from mooring close enough to step ashore. In SE winds, one should try to moor here as the NW quay is exposed.

In 1984 the NE part of the harbour was being dredged.

Alternatively, yachts may anchor in the bay adjacent to the harbour, where there is a large area with depths from 3 m to 12 m on a bottom of weed and sand, but this is wide open to E and SE.

In the harbour one may be asked to pay a mooring fee, which, at over £2 (1984) even if only staying for one night, was rather more than the cost of a room for the night in the village!

Facilities

🛢 ⚓ ❄ £ ✉ ⌐ ✐ ⌐ plus officials for a Port of Entry.

There are several restaurants, bars and cafés. Water is available on the quay, but fuel can only be collected by canister in a taxi from the village of Datça.

Bottled gas is only available in Turkish type bottles.

Minibuses (Dolmuş) run regularly to Marmaris.

INCE BURUN   36°39'.7N 27°40'.5E   (No plan)

Immediately N of the Ince Burun lighthouse is a triangular bay, open to the E, barren and unattractive, but providing a possibly useful protection from a strong blow from the W. Anchor on weed and sand, with some rock patches to be avoided, and take a stern line to a rock to the W if desired. Depths are 4–12 m.

Datça Iskelesi

100m
scale approx.

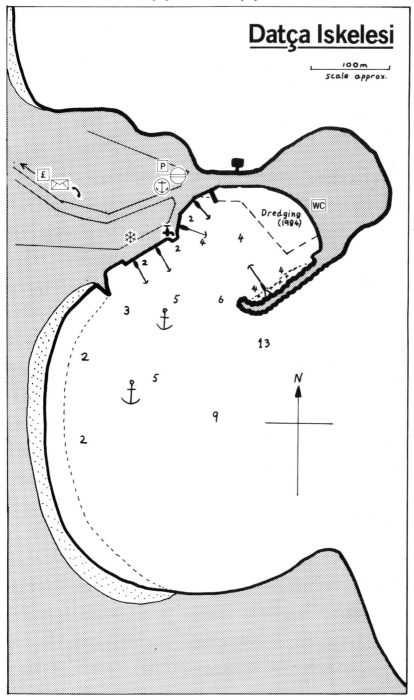

Dredging
(1984)

WC

N

OVA BÜKÜ   36°41′.1N 27°34′.5E   (No plan)

A reasonably well-protected anchorage, open to the S quadrant. The entrance to the bay is easily identified as the cliff to the E of it is of brown rock, while that to the W is light grey. There is a metal frame lookout tower on top of the E side of the mouth. There is also one on the W side, but not so clearly visible.

Inside, there is a rocky projection in the shore between two beaches to the NE and NW, and one can anchor off either of these. Off the NE beach the bottom is rocky but with sand patches, and depths are 4–8 m. To the NW, depths are 3–6 m on sand, although this too becomes rocky to the extreme W. A short stone mole projects NE from the W side of the bay.

Caution: From the rocky projection between the two beaches dangerous underwater rocks extend for about 100 m to the south, so great care should be taken to skirt around these if moving from one side of the bay to the other.

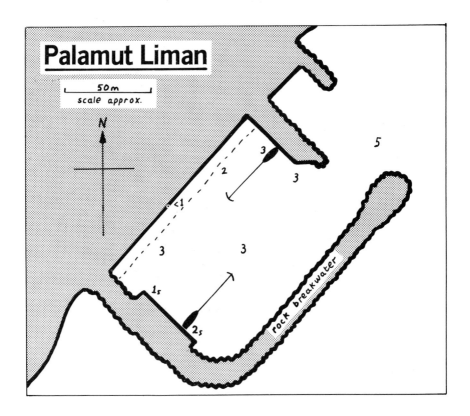

PALAMUT LIMAN   36°40′.2N 27°30′.2E

An unexpected and useful little harbour, recently made and still rather untidy, with breakwaters of large stone boulders. It provides practically all-round protection, but there are no facilities, and only a few houses on the shore. Some more building is clearly in progress, including a seasonal restaurant and café. Moor stern-to the concreted parts of the breakwater, as marked on the plan. Approach with caution in strong SE'ly winds.

KNIDOS   36°41′.1N 27°27′.5E

Site of the ancient town of Knidos, on the western tip of the Datça peninsula. To the NE of the isthmus dividing the old silted harbour to the NW from the present one to the SE are the ruins of a number of buildings of various kinds, and a quite well preserved amphitheatre. Now there are just a few summer restaurants, and a customs post looking out for boats sailing from the Greek islands which have not cleared into Turkey.

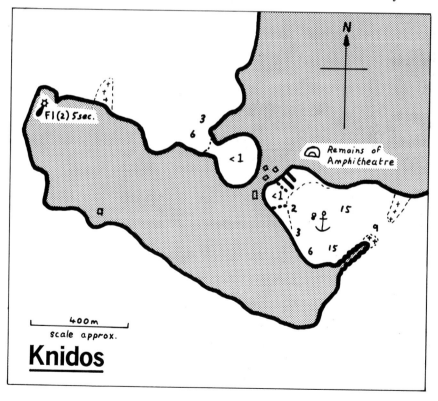

Knidos

Mooring

Being right on the end of the peninsula, Knidos has a reputation for being rather windy, and having poor holding ground. Certainly when winds are strong, the holding, on a bottom of weed and sand, is not always sufficient. Although partially open to SE there is practically all round protection from the swell. If a SE wind should blow, one can moor tight up behind the SE breakwater with stern lines to the large rocks from which it is constructed.

Enter fairly close to the end of the breakwater to be well clear of the now submerged mole projecting from the N shore opposite.

Depths are between 7 m and 15 m, shallowing to less than 2 m towards the head of the bay, in the area of several wooden jetties in various states of disrepair.

CHAPTER 7

Gulf of Kos (Gökova Körfezi)

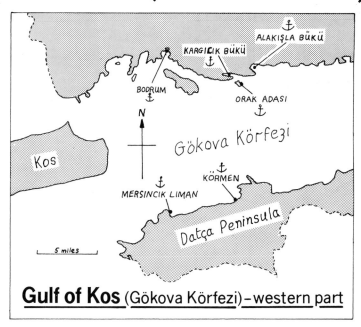

Gulf of Kos (Gökova Körfezi) – western part

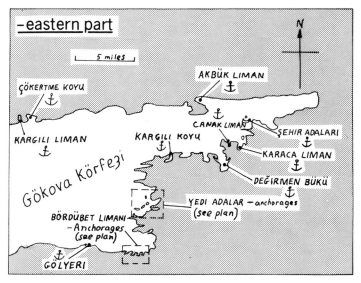

Harbours and anchorages

	Open to:	Comments:
Southern shore (from West to East)		
Mersincik Liman	NE/E	–
Körmen (harbour)	–	Entrance difficult in strong N/NW winds
Gölyeri	NE/E	–
Bördübet Limani anchorages		
(a)	E	–
(b)	N/NE	–
(c)	N	All round shelter for small-medium size yachts
(d)	NW/N	–
(e)	W/NW/N	–
(f)	W/NW/N	Westerly swell enters
Yedi Adalar anchorages		
(a)	E	For short fetch. Some rebound swell in W/NW'ly winds
(b) Karaağac	W	Some protection from W behind spur at entrance
(c)	–	–
Kargili Koyu	–	–
Değirmen Bükü	–	–
Canak Liman	N	–
Karaca Liman	N	–
Şehir Adalari	NE	Some rebound swell in strong W'ly winds
Northern shore anchorages (from East to West)		
Akbük Liman	E/SE	–
Çökertme Koyu	S/SE	Some rebound swell in SW'ly winds
Kargili Liman	SW/S/SE	–
Alakişla Bükü	S/SE/E	–
Orak Adasi	N	Only for 1 mile fetch
Kargicik Bükü	E/SE	–
Bodrum (marina, Port of Entry)	–	Poor in very strong S/SE'ly winds

GULF OF KOS – SOUTHERN SHORE

MERSINCIK LIMAN   36°45'.3N 27°28'.6E   (No plan)

This is the most westerly refuge on the southern shore of the gulf from a west wind, before reaching Knidos at the tip of the Datça peninsula. It lies 1 mile SSE from the islet, Akçali Adasi, and the best position for anchoring is in the tiny cove on the NW side of the mouth of the bay. (The main body of the bay itself is about $\frac{1}{2}$ mile wide, rather open and subject to swell.) In this small cove, however, with a pebble beach at its head, one can anchor in 3–7 m (on sand with some stones), and run out a stern line to a rock as there is not sufficient room to swing. Open only to the E.

KÖRMEN   36°46'.3N 27°37'E

A rather desolate and isolated spot, but with a harbour of stone break-waters that provides all round shelter. It lies $2\frac{1}{2}$ miles SW of Ince Burnu (Cape Shuyun) lighthouse, towards the SW end of a stretch of fertile low-lying coastline, and in front of a small white-painted café, one of the only buildings in sight.

With a swell from very strong W to N winds, the approach to the harbour would be difficult, if not impossible, as a sharp turn is required into the entrance to avoid running ashore on the beach.

Moor stern-to in the inner or outer harbour where shown on the plan, but because of the irregular rubble of the breakwater foundations, it may be difficult to get close enough to step ashore. The inner harbour is better sheltered from all directions than the outer one. There is however a concrete quay to the SW side of the outer harbour where one can moor alongside. This is occasionally used by commercial coasters. Otherwise, the only other craft in the place are a few small local fishing boats.

The small café on the beach may serve basic meals of fish, in summer.

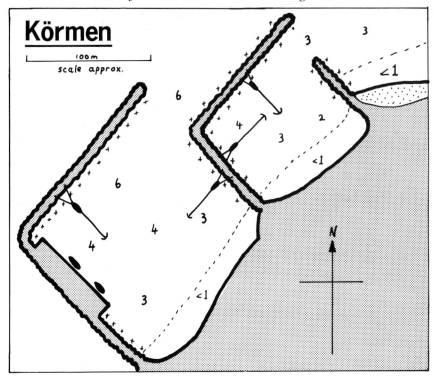

GÖLYERI   36°48'.6N 27°53'.7E   (No plan)

This small, quite open bay, lying about half way up the gulf on the southern shore, is often used by fishing boats as a night anchorage to gain useful shelter from the west.

To identify the bay, which is not very clear, Koyun Burun lighthouse point should be on a bearing of 038°T. Anchor in 4–8 m on sand and light weed. Open to the NE quadrant.

BÖRDÜBET LIMANI – Anchorages

Here, in the extreme SE corner of the gulf are several small, secluded, and some very attractive and well-sheltered inlets, on the southern shore. In one or other, protection can be gained from almost any direction, except possibly a strong northerly blow.

Caution: There are rocks low-lying and awash at various points close offshore in the area of these inlets, and careful attention

should be paid to the plan, and charts. Also, note the area of only 2 m depth at the mouth of the eastern-most inlet of the group.

From west to east:

Anchorage (a)   36°48′N 27°59′.6E
The western-most of these inlets, very narrow at its head, with a gently shelving sea-bed, and anchorage in 5–10 m on sand and light weed. A stern line could be taken to a tree. Open to the E, but well protected from the W.

Anchorage (b)   36°47′.7N 28°00′.5E
Shallow at the head; fairly good shelter, but open to N; 3–12 m depth on sand and light weed, with a stern line to a tree on the W shore.

Anchorage (c)   36°47′.5N 28°00′.9E
Very good, practically all-round shelter in the SW corner; pine wooded shores, attractive and peaceful, but quite often used by fishing boats as an overnight anchorage; 2–6 m depths on mud and sand with light weed; a stern line can be taken to a tree; shallow in the extreme SW.

Anchorage (d)   36°47′.5N 28°01′.3E
Not as well protected from the west as (c), but otherwise very pleasant; 3–11 m depths, on sand and light weed; keep clear of rocks close to east shore.

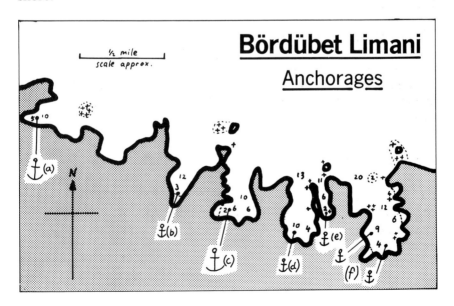

Bördübet Limani
Anchorages

Anchorage (e)   36°47'.5N 28°01'.4E
A narrow inlet with only fair protection; 2–6 m depth on sand; a stern line
to a tree will be required.

Anchorage (f)   36°47'.4N 28°02'E
More open to westerly swell; 3–12 m depths on sand; shallow in some of
the coves off the main bay as shown on the plan; keep to the W of the area
with only 2 m depth at the mouth of the inlet.

YEDI ADALAR – Anchorages

This stretch of coast, partially protected from the west by the three large
and one very small islet comprising the Yedi Adalar group, provides some
pleasant anchorages, quite well sheltered but not in all conditions, as

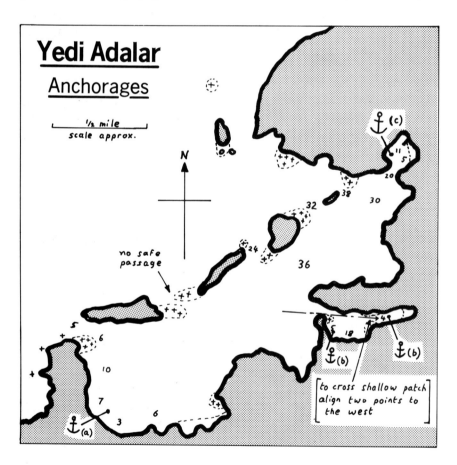

explained. Pay careful attention to charts, and the plan, for rocks close to the surface and awash, and for safe passages between the islets.

Anchorage (a)   36°51′.6N 28°01′.3E

Here, in the SW corner off the beach, shelter is quite good from all directions, only a swell working round from the NW would make it uncomfortable. Anchor in 3–8 m, on sand with some weed; a stern line could be taken to a tree on the west or south-west shore, particularly as a precaution in strong westerly winds.

Anchorage (b)   Karaağac   36°52′N 28°03′E

A very narrow inlet extending to the east, with anchorage in 6–10 m, either immediately around to the right as you enter behind the isthmus (where there is one tree suitable for a stern line), or possibly further into the inlet beyond the shallow patch shown on the plan.

The inlet is, however, a funnel for westerly winds, and if these are strong, a yacht needs heavy ground tackle to maintain position. Also, some swell may enter.

Anchorage (c)   36°47′.5N 28°00′.9E

Probably offers the best all round protection. In strong westerly winds tuck tight in around to the left as you enter, and take a stern line to a tree. Depths are 6–14 m, and the bottom is gravel and mud which can be difficult holding in parts.

KARGILI KOYU   36°56′.1N 28°05′.9E

A completely enclosed secluded narrow inlet, 3½ miles E of Koyun Burun lighthouse, providing excellent anchorage for small and medium sized yachts, in pine-wooded lake-like surroundings.

The entrance is not easily seen from any distance away, and is best pin-pointed by taking a bearing on the Karaburun peninsula on the opposite shore of the gulf.

The better mooring is towards the very head of the inlet, but to reach here one has to cross a shallow patch of silt with less than 2 m depth over it. Note that one should proceed with some caution as the silting changes from year to year and may not be quite as shown on the plan.

Once across the shallow patch, depths are around 2 m, and a small yacht may have just enough room to anchor and swing, or a stern line could be run out to a tree on the N shore. Bottom is mud, but with some

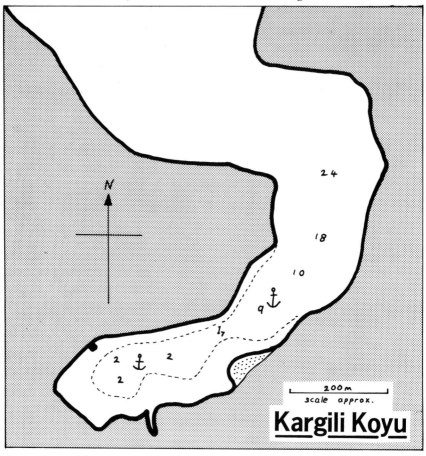

weed, waterlogged sticks and twigs, and rubbish, which may prevent an anchor from biting first time.

Yachts unable to cross the shallow patch should anchor where the 9–10 m depths are shown on the plan. Here also a stern line could be taken to a tree on the N shore. Small fishing boats sometimes spend the night here, but otherwise the place is quiet, peaceful, and the only sign of habitation is a small farm house nearby.

DEĞIRMEN BÜKÜ   36°55′N 28°10′E

Here a yacht can anchor with all round shelter in any of three different parts of this reasonably large inlet.

Tucked right around in the NW corner is the so-called English

Değirmen Bükü

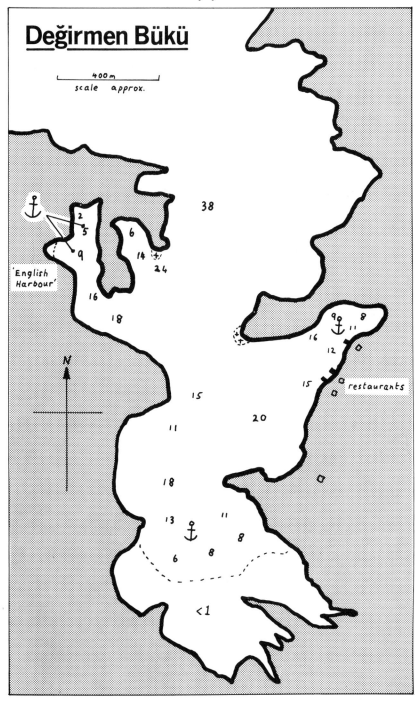

400m
scale approx.

38

2
5
6
9
14
24

'English
Harbour'

16

18

15

N

11

20

18

13   11
8
6   8

<1

9 8
11
16
12
15   restaurants

harbour, I would hope not named merely for being dull and unattractive, which it unfortunately is! Shelter is good from all directions, although swinging room is limited. There are a few trees to which a stern line could be taken. Anchoring depths are 4–10 m on sand with light weed.

At the extreme south of the inlet is anchorage in 6–15 m on mud, with ample room to swing for larger yachts. The very head of the bay is silted, as shown on the plan. There can be some swell here in strong W/NW winds.

By far the most attractive part of Değirmen Bükü is the arm extending to NE. Here is all round shelter in wooded surroundings, with anchorage in 8–16 m on mud and weed, with trees suitable for a stern line to the NE and NW.

There are a few simple summer restaurants on the eastern shore, and spring water is available, but expensive.

CANAK LIMAN   36°56'.9N 28°10'.4E   (No plan)

Just to the NE of the mouth of Değirmen Bükü is this tiny narrow inlet extending southwards, providing very good shelter for a small or medium sized yacht. There is deep water at the entrance, and as one approaches the head of the inlet, it divides into two parts, with a fishery area to the SW. Avoiding this, anchor in 3–6 m on sand with a stern line to a tree or rock. In the extreme SE part the depth is less than 2 m. The anchorage is narrowly open to N.

KARACA LIMAN   36°56'.6N 28°11'.3E   (No plan)

A pleasant and fairly well sheltered anchorage, in a bay extending S off the main body of Karaca Liman, 3 miles just W of S from Sehir Adalari. A small villa development can be seen in the trees at the head of the cove, with two wooden jetties extending out from the shore.

To escape most of a swell from the W, moor to the W side of the bay, either off the olive grove or a little to the S of it. The sea-bed is quite steep-to, and a stern line should be taken to a tree. Depths are 15–18 m, on sand.

ŞEHIR ADALARI   36°59'.7N 28°12'.5E

The larger of these two islands is popularly known as Cleopatra's Island

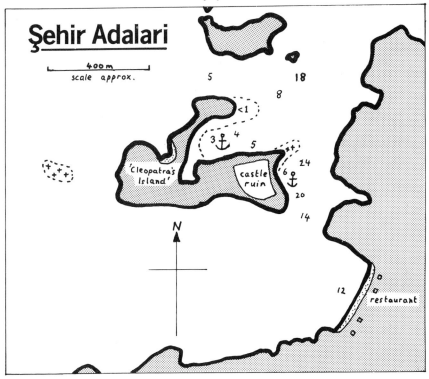

and has the remains of a castle and an amphitheatre on its E side. An attractive spot from the sea, but even more so from the island, with a beach of beautiful white sand.

In the two areas marked for anchoring on the plan, shelter is only fair. In strong west winds, the swell will rebound off the mainland shore causing some disturbance. Immediately to the east of the castle, the bottom is sand and light weed, and quite steep-to. A stern line could be taken to a rock or tree on the island.

To NW of the castle, there is room to swing, with depths of 3–6 m on sand. Here also a stern line could be run out to a rock or tree to the west.

There is a small seasonal restaurant on the mainland beach to the SE.

Caution: Shallow areas extend out between the anchorages, and also south-eastward from the northern tip of the island. Also, note the rocks awash approximately 400 m to the west.

GULF OF KOS – NORTHERN SHORE

AKBÜK LIMAN   37°01'.8N 28°06'E   (No plan)

This is the eastern-most anchorage on the north shore of the gulf. It is a large, attractive and deep bay, with olive groves on the north shore, and impressive steep mountain slopes behind.

To WNW is a long stony beach, with a small summer café towards the southern end. Anchor off either end of the beach in 6–14 m on sand and light weed. In the centre it is less suitable as the sea-bed is more steep-to. In the extreme SW, depths are shallow.

Alternatively anchor off one of the tiny coves on the S shore, 500–800 m before reaching the head of the bay. Some are rather shallow close in, but one can anchor in 3–8 m and take a stern line to a rock or tree.

Well protected from the W, but open to the SE quadrant.

ÇÖKERTME KOYU   37°00'.3N 27°47'.3E   (No plan)

Close to the tiny village of Çökertme is a reasonably well sheltered anchorage to either north or south on the west side of the bay (anchorage off the village itself is rather steep-to and exposed). In the N corner, depths are 3–10 m on sand and stones, and to the south-west, 4–12 m on mud and weed.

The bay is exposed to the S, and some swell from a strong W or E wind will work its way into the anchorage.

There is also a tiny cove right on the tip of the W side of the mouth of the bay, open to the E, but offering shelter from the W for one or two boats, anchoring on a stone and sand bottom in 4–10 m with a stern line to a rock to the W.

There are one or two small restaurants in the village, and one may see carpets being woven in the traditional way.

KARGILI LIMAN   37°00'N 27°46'.6E   (No plan)

A pleasant inlet ½ mile long lying immediately W of Çökertme, open to the S quadrant. Anchor at the head, just off the beach with a scattering of olive trees and a small area of fertile ground behind. The bottom is gently shelving, fine sand and light weed, and depths are 4–10 m. Room to swing, but a stern line could be taken to a tree on shore to the W. Swell from strong W winds will work into the bay, but not severely.

ALAKIŞLA BÜKÜ   36°59'.1N 27°38'.5E   (No plan)

Immediately north of Karaburun point, and 2½ miles east of Orak Adasi, this anchorage is protected from W but wide open to E and SE. A rock stands a few metres high in the cove, close to the shore, but there is room to anchor beside it in 4–14 m on sand with stones if one secures the stern with a line to a rock on shore.

Caution: Take care to avoid the rocks awash between Karaburun point and the small islet Yildiz Adasi to the east of the point.

ORAK ADASI   36°58'.8N 27°35'.6E   (No plan)

A secluded spot in an attractive cove on the N shore of the islet Orak Adasi. There is a stone hut with a tiny stone jetty in front of it at the head of the cove, and a small beach in front of an olive grove.

Anchor in 4–14 m on firm sand with stones, and run out a stern line to a rock or tree as there is not room to swing.

Reasonable shelter from all directions, with only a 1 mile fetch across to the mainland coast to the north.

KARGICIK BÜKÜ   36°59'.3N 27°33'.8E   (No plan)

Popularly known also as Papuji Bay, this large inlet lies 8 miles ESE from Bodrum, 1½ miles WNW of Orak Adasi. There is a stony beach at the head, and a large area to anchor with depths of 4–12 m on a bottom of sand with light weed. Shelter from the W and N is good, but the bay is open to swell from E or SE.

A pleasant spot, but tends to be popular in summer being only a short sail from Bodrum.

BODRUM   37°02'.2N 27°25'.5E   Port of Entry

A fine, modern, thriving holiday town, with an impressive medieval castle standing proudly on the headland between the large harbour to the west and a wide bay to the east.

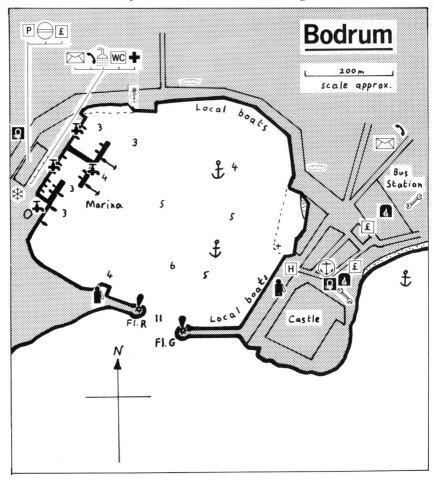

The castle is well worth a visit, and also the ancient amphitheatre on the hillside to the north with a superb view across to the castle and eastwards up the gulf. On the north shore of off-lying Karaada island there are interesting warm springs in a cave situated next to a hotel.

Mooring

On entering the harbour between the two breakwaters, the marine is around to the left. Moor as directed by the berthing master who may attract your attention with a whistle. Inner berths are provided with individual strops from a ground chain to secure to the bows, with stern

The amphitheatre, Bodrum

lines to the concrete pontoons. Larger yachts on the outer berths use their own ground tackle to go stern-to.

Berthing fees are priced in US dollars, thereby keeping pace with the considerable Turkish rate of inflation, although one pays in local currency. While they are (1984) cheap for larger boats ($9 per day for a 70-footer) for small boats they seem disproportionately expensive ($5 per day for a 24-footer). One also has to pay for a minimum three day period, somewhat irksome if only making a short visit as part of a two week cruise. I even found the staff uncertain whether to charge by the night, or by the day or part thereof.

The walls of the town quay are reserved only for local boats, but you can anchor free in the eastern part of the harbour in 4–5 m, weed on mud, keeping well away from the very long anchor lines of the local 'gulets' (cruising boats of traditional design).

In strong NW summer winds, a better anchorage is in the bay to the E of the castle, off the beach, but this is of course wide open to the S. The wind here appears less strong than in the harbour, which always seems to accelerate a NW'ly blow.

In strong SE winds, even the marina and the harbour can become uncomfortable. There is talk of a new wall to give more protection from the S, but this still seems a long way off.

Building the traditional 'gulets' at Güllük

Facilities

🕯 🔩 🔥 ❄ £ 🔌 🔧 ⚓ ✚ Ⓓ ✉ ⌇ 🗡 ⌒ 🚿 ▢

Officials for a Port of Entry are in the marina, and one should moor there if entering from abroad as anchoring off will cause suspicion.

Water and electricity points are provided in the marina, and charged extra. In summer, water may only be on for an hour a day, and one has to watch for the marina staff watering the flowers to know when this time will be! Showers are rather insufficient (2 for men, 2 for women) and hot water is solar heated, so what little there is is only available on warm sunny days! Washing machines, although advertised, had still not been installed in 1984.

Note that it is not possible in Bodrum to take on water except at the marina, and to do so, one has to pay the marina mooring fee.

Bottled gas is mainly Turkish, but one can find European type bottles in town.

There is an inter-city bus terminus serving all parts of Turkey, and a ferry service runs regularly to Kos in summer, and according to demand in the winter.

As a place to winter, the marina provides rather poor shelter. The surge in SE gales can be rather alarming, and the mooring strops have been known to break, and the ground chains to move. One hopes the situation will be improved.

Hauling out facilities in the yards along the coast nearby are rather poor, and not recommended for sailing yachts. The small boatyard in the harbour is being steadily run down to make way some time in the future for hard standing and piers for a Travel Hoist.

Note: The rocks off Harem Burun point, 1¼ miles SSW of Bodrum harbour are marked by a small black buoy which is hard to spot in rough weather.

Passage is not possible between the islet Görecek Adasi (3 miles SW of Bodrum) and the mainland shore.

CHAPTER 8

Bodrum to Mandalya Gulf

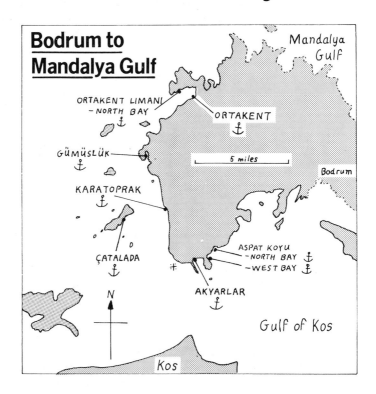

Bodrum to Mandalya Gulf

ORTAKENT LIMANI
– NORTH BAY

ORTAKENT

GÜMÜSLÜK

5 miles

Bodrum

KARATOPRAK

ASPAT KOYU
– NORTH BAY
– WEST BAY

ÇATALADA

AKYARLAR

N

Gulf of Kos

Kos

Mandalya Gulf

Harbours and anchorages

	Open to:	*Comments*:
Aspat Koyu, North bay	S/SE/E	–
Aspat Koyu, West bay	S/SE/E	–
Akyarlar	S/SE	–
Çatalada (Pirasa Adasi)	S/SE/E	–
Karatoprak	–	Draught limited to 2 m Difficult entrance in strong SW/W/NW'ly winds
Gümüslük	S/SW	–
Ortakent	–	Draught limited to 2 m
Ortakent Limani, North bay	SW/S/SE	Only for 1 mile fetch

ASPAT KOYU – North bay   36°58′.4N 27°18′.2E   (No plan)

One of two coves in Aspat Koyu, 6½ miles SW of Bodrum, suitable for anchoring in certain conditions. Here in the northern bay there is a small deserted stone house on shore, and a stream runs out at the east end of the beach. Protection from W and NW is good, but the bay is wide open to the SE quadrant. Anchor in 2–6 m on a very gently shelving bottom of soft sand.

ASPAT KOYU – West bay   36°58′.4N 27°18′.2E   (No plan)

Anchorage to the south of the white villa complex where there is a sandy beach with a few summer restaurants, and one or two wooden jetties. The bottom is very gently shelving (2 m depth 100 m off the beach), sand, and depths are 2–5 m. Protected from W, but wide open from NE to SE.

AKYARLAR   35°58′N 27°17′.2E   (No plan)

The last refuge from a west wind before leaving the Gulf of Kos. On the tip of the headland on the W side of the mouth of the bay is a lookout tower, and a stone building.

In the NE part of the bay there is an L-shaped rock breakwater in front of the minaret, projecting SE and E, where the maximum depth is only 2 m close behind it. A small boat could moor with a line to a rock on the breakwater. There is a military post and a few small restaurants on shore.

Alternatively anchor to the NW, off a beach with a few villas and a customs post. Depths are 2–6 m, on sand and weed.

This is not an attractive spot, and is only useful to gain some shelter from the west, although NW winds tend to be stronger and more gusty here than after one leaves the gulf.

ÇATALADA (Pirasa Adasi)   37°00′.4N 27°13′.2E   (No plan)

Çatalada looks like two islands, but there is a very low-lying isthmus between the two parts. The anchorage is on the SE side of this isthmus in 2–7 m on a very gently shelving bottom of sand and light weed. Open to S and SE, but good and useful protection from NW.

KARATOPRAK   37°00′.4N 27°15′.4E

A pleasant little village with a small harbour, but deep enough only for small or shallow draft yachts. A nice sandy beach is just to the north of the harbour.

Mooring

The entrance to the harbour, in front of a conspicuous minaret, is from the south. Maximum depth is approximately 1.8 m. Moor bows-to or stern-to where shown on the plan. Keep close to the harbour breakwater approaching the entrance, as there is shallow water to the south.

With a swell from a wind in the west quadrant, approach might be impossible, as a yacht may bump on the bottom in the troughs.

Practically all-round shelter, but partly open to the south.

Facilities

Several restaurants and cafés, shops for provisions, and a baker. There is also a bus station with connections to the inter-city bus routes.

Caution: If approaching from the north, be careful to skirt wide around the shallow area that extends some distance to NW of the harbour.

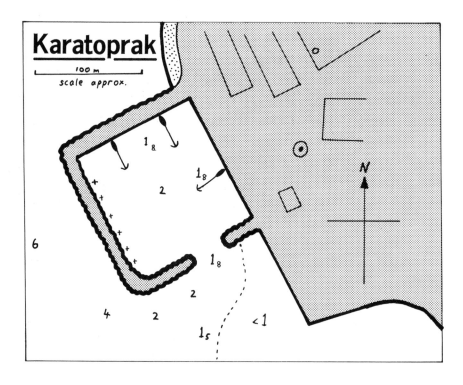

GÜMÜSLÜK   37°03'.4N 27°14'E

A very attractive anchorage, but rather popular in the season, with a small community and several pretty summer restaurants around the shore.

Anchor anywhere in the bay in 6–18 m on mud and weed. A stern line is not advisable if the place is crowded, as yachts anchored out may swing into a yacht held by the stern during the night.

Very good, almost all-round shelter, but partially open to the south past the island at the mouth.

Caution: Off Karabakla Burun point, 1 mile S of Gümüslük, there are rocks barely above water close W of some that are clearly visible. One should keep well clear.

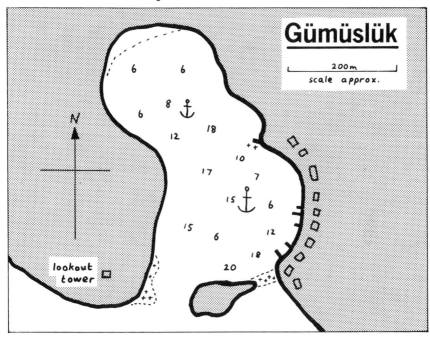

ORTAKENT   37°06'.5N 27°17'.5E

This small unspoilt little village appears to have hardly any visitors except the occasional small yacht.

Mooring

The harbour, created by two rock breakwaters, provides all-round protection, but the depths are only 2 m. Moor bow- or stern-to the concreted walls, or in a strong westerly blow moor with lines to the west breakwater, but stand off a little to avoid the uneven foundations underwater close in.

Facilities

A couple of small restaurants provide simple food, most likely of local fish. Minibuses run from here to Bodrum.

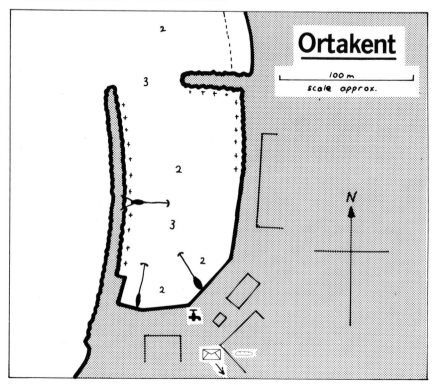

Caution: Shallow water extends some ½ mile out from the shore ½ mile west of Ortakent harbour. Approaching one should therefore keep well offshore until NW of the harbour, before turning towards it.

ORTAKENT LIMANI – North bay   37°07′.1N 27°16′.3E   (No plan)

On the other side of the small gulf from Ortakent harbour is this unnamed cove providing a reasonable and secluded anchorage, close by a few scattered villas on the shore to the NE. The shore to the west is barren and gently sloping. Anchor in 4–10 m, weed on sand. Good protection from NW, and open to SE only for a short 1 mile fetch across to Ortakent village.

CHAPTER 9

Mandalya Gulf (Güllük Körfezi)

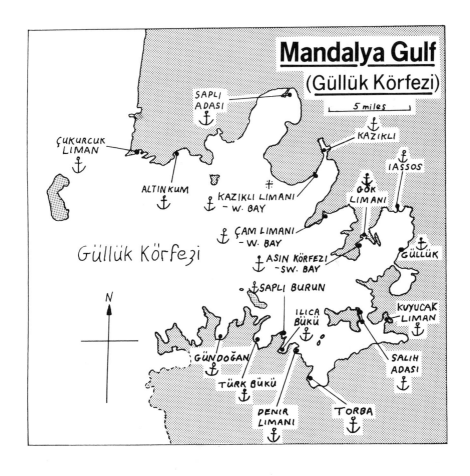

Mandalya Gulf

(Güllük Körfezi)

5 miles

SAPLI ADASI

ÇUKURCUK LIMAN

KAZIKLI

IASSOS

ALTINKUM

KAZIKLI LIMANI – W. BAY

GÖK LIMANI

ÇAM LIMANI – W. BAY

Güllük Körfezi

ASIN KÖRFEZI – SW. BAY

GÜLLÜK

SAPLI BURUN

N

ILICA BÜKÜ

KUYUCAK LIMAN

GÜNDOĞAN

SALIH ADASI

TÜRK BÜKÜ

DENIR LIMANI

TORBA

Harbours and anchorages

	Open to:	Comments:
Gündoğan	N	Difficult approach in strong N'ly winds. Draught limited to 2 m
Türk Bükü	NE/E	More protection behind breakwater for small–medium size yachts
Sapli Burun	E/SE	–
Ilica Bükü	N/NE	–
Denir Limani	NE/E	–
Torba	–	–
Kuyucak Liman	–	Some swell in strong SW'ly winds
Salih Adasi, South bay	S/SE/E	Only for 1–2 mile fetch
Salih Adasi, North bay	S	–
Güllük (harbour) Port of Entry	W/NW/N	More protection for small–medium size yachts behind breakwater
Iassos	S	–
Gök Limani	S/SE	–
Asin Körfezi, West bay	S/SE/E	–
Çam Limani, West bay	S/SE/E	–
Kazikli	S	–
Kazikli Limani, West bay	S/SE/E	Only for 1–2 mile fetch
Sapli Adasi	SW/S	–
Altinkum (Karakuyu Koyu)	S/SE/E	–
Çukurcuk Liman	SW/S/SE	–

GÜNDOĞAN   37°08′N 27°20′.8E   (No plan)

This is the most westward of the anchorages on the southern side of the gulf, offering limited shelter for small yachts at the head of the inlet behind a rock L-shaped breakwater projecting N and E. Approach to the left hand end of the breakwater, and turn sharply in behind it, in front of the beach.

Here is a small community in an agreeable setting, with a couple of summer restaurants on shore close by, and very few visitors.

There are maximum 2 m depths to moor bows-to the N or W

breakwater, but no mooring points, only rocks to tie off lines. The bottom shallows up to the beach on the S side of the harbour.

Although protected from all around, the approach to this harbour is open to the N, and should not be attempted in very strong northerly winds.

TÜRK BÜKÜ   37°07′.9N 27°22′.7E   (No plan)

A spacious bay with plenty of area for anchoring, less than a mile SW of Büyük Adasi island. Anchor anywhere near the shore to the west, on a gently shelving bottom of weed and sand, in depths of 5–15 m. The setting is attractive with a few small houses scattered on the hills around, and one or two seasonal restaurants on shore.

Towards the south side is a small rocky breakwater projecting west, which affords protection from the N and E, otherwise, the anchorage is open to E and NE but well sheltered from SW to NW. Lines could be taken to the breakwater, and depths behind it are from 5 m at the outer end to 2 m towards the root. One should not moor too close to the breakwater itself as the rocky foundations are uneven.

SAPLI BURUN   37°08′N 27°24′.6E   (No plan)

A small very secluded cove on the east side of Sapli Burun point, $1\frac{1}{2}$ miles E of Türk Bükü, with a beach at its head. Depths are 7–15 m on sand and weed, with a stern line possible to a rock on shore to the NW. Open only to E.

ILICA BÜKÜ   37°07′.2N 27°25′.1E   (No plan)

An attractive and secluded inlet $2\frac{1}{4}$ miles E of Turk Bükü, open only to the N, with densely wooded slopes all around. The bottom is rather steep-to, and one should anchor towards the head in 15–20 m, running out a stern line to a tree on the W shore. In the extreme SW corner depths are less, 4–9 m. The bottom is sand and weed. Some swell will work into the inlet from a NW wind.

DENIR LIMANI   37°07'.2N 27°26'E   (No plan)

A small inlet 3 miles WSW of Salih Adasi island, with only a couple of small dwellings at its head.

The bottom is gently shelving, 5–15 m anchoring depths on sand and weed, with room to swing, or a stern line could be run out to a rock or bush on the NW shore. Open to E and NE.

TORBA   37° 05'.3N 27°27'.4E

A charming little harbour with all-round protection beside a small community of a few well-kept private villas with colourful flowered gardens. There is one summer restaurant, and the road to Bodrum passes close by.

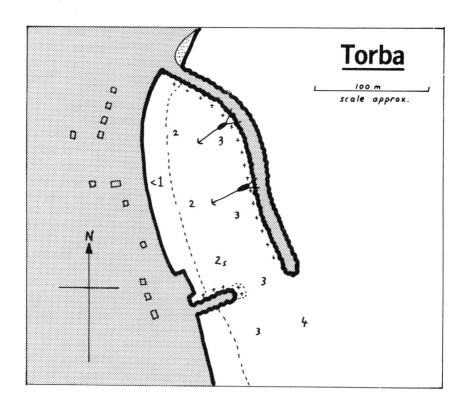

The breakwater is of piled rocks, and coming bows-to or stern-to one should stand a little way off to avoid the uneven foundations. Lines can only be tied off to rocks as there are no mooring points.

KUYUCAK LIMAN   37°09'.4N 27°33'.3E   (No plan)

A well-protected and uninhabited inlet, close E of the island Salih Adasi. Facing you as you come in through the entrance, is a stone ruin on the NE shore. To the SE of this, the bay is unfortunately too silted and shallow for most boats to anchor. Towards the NW, there are 2–6 m depths on sand, with trees on the W shore suitable for a stern line if desired. The sea-bed shelves to less than 2 m some way from the extreme NW shore. A quiet, secluded anchorage.

SALIH ADASI – South bay   37°09'.1N 27°32'E   (No plan)

The first of two coves on the east side of the island suitable for anchoring. A white villa with a small private quay stands on the shores on the north side of the cove. The bottom is gently shelving sand, 3–10 m, and a stern line could be run out to a rock or tree to the west. Open only to S and SE across a short 2 mile fetch to Güvercinlik Körfezi.

SALIH ADASI – North bay   37°09'.7N 27°32'.1E   (No plan)

Good protection in a small cove at the narrowest point of the channel between Salih Adasi and the mainland. Olive groves stand all around, and a stone wall runs along the shore to the NW with a few small stone buildings behind it. Anchor in 6–10 m on sand. Open only for a short 2 mile fetch to the S.

GÜLLÜK   37°14'.3N 27°35'.7E   Port of entry

A poor small harbour, and a rather unattractive town, but a Port of Entry with some facilities.

Mooring
Small boats could go bows-to amongst the fishing boats on the W wall in the harbour. Depths are greater towards the outer end of the rock

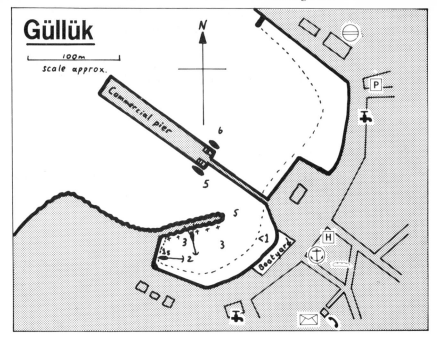

Güllük

breakwater, but there are no mooring points, foundations below the surface are uneven, and scope for a stern anchor across the harbour is limited.

Yachts calling only to complete entry or exit formalities can moor alongside the steps half-way along the commercial jetty, but not with a swell from SW or NW winds.

Facilities

⚓ ✉ 〜 ↰ plus officials for a Port of Entry.

There are a few restaurants, and shops for essential provisions. Buses run to nearby towns with connections to the main routes.

IASSOS   37°16'.6N 27°34'.9E

This is the site of the ancient town of Iassos, but few ruins remain, apart from the castle on the headland on the east side of the bay. At the head is a

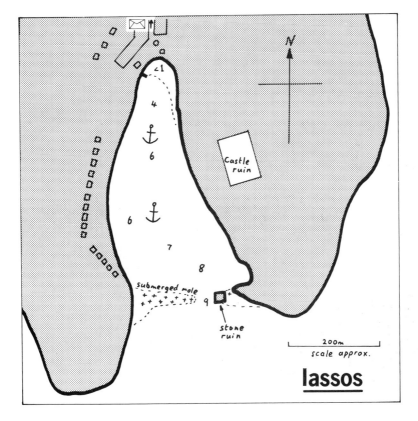

small village with a conspicuous minaret. On the ridge on the W side are a line of rather unattractive chalets.

Mooring

There are convenient anchoring depths of 4–10 m over the whole area of the bay on mud with some weed, and room to swing. Protection is good from almost all directions, but the inlet is open to the S, and in W or even NW prevailing winds a swell may enter coming up the gulf from SW.

To avoid the ancient submerged mole extending out from the west side of the entrance, enter well to the right hand side, close to the square stone ruin standing in the water.

Facilities

One very simple summer restaurant.

GÖK LIMANI   37°15'N 27°13'.1E   (No plan)

An isolated inlet 3 miles west of Güllük on the opposite shore of the gulf Asim Körfezi. As you enter there is small islet to the right, and then, once inside, the main body of the bay bends around to the NE, where one can anchor in about 4 m. Depths before turning into the NE part are greater, 9–14 m. The bottom is mud, and the water murky, so one should not approach the shore too closely as it is silted and shallow in parts, particularly in the extreme NE, and immediately N of the islet, where passage is not possible. Open only to SE.

ASIN KÖRFEZI – South-west bay   37°14'.4N 27°31'.4E
(No plan)

An open bay, but a pleasant secluded anchorage, 3¾ miles E of Güllük across the gulf, 1 mile SW of Gök Limani. There are olive groves on the hillside to the SW, and a tiny cottage stands on the left hand end of the beach. Anchor on a gently shelving bottom of sand and weed in 3–12 m. A stern line could be run out to a tree on the shore to the west. Open to E and SE.

ÇAM LIMANI – West bay   37°16'.1N 27°28'.8E   (No plan)

Not particularly attractive, but a wild and secluded anchorage, lying 2½ miles NNW of Incegöl Burnu point and lighthouse. There is a small beach at the head of the inlet to the NW, and olive groves behind. Anchor off the beach on a gently shelving bottom of mud and light weed, in 4–15 m with room to swing. A stern line could be taken to a rock to the west. Open to the SE quadrant, but can also be subject to swell running up from SW in W or NW winds.

KAZIKLI 37°20'.3N 27°28'.6E

A large inlet extending NNW from the head of the gulf Kazikli Limani, with olive groves around the shores, and only a few small dwellings here and there. There are convenient anchoring depths over most of the inlet,

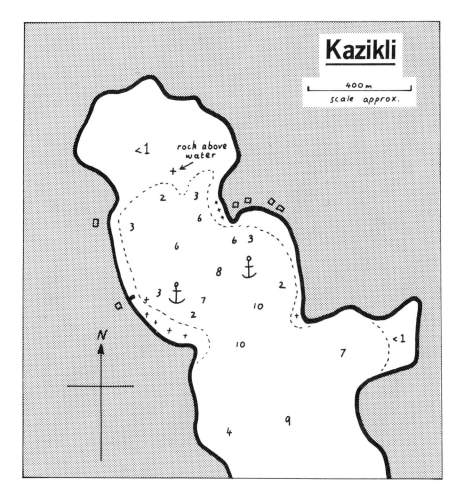

as shown on the plan, except where it is silted and very shallow at the head. In 1984 the limit of this area was marked by an above water pile of stones. The bottom is mud, and the water murky.

Open only to the S.

KAZIKLI LIMANI – West bay   37°19'.2N 27°28'.1E   (No plan)

Rather more open but a more attractive pine wooded anchorage in this small unnamed cove 1 mile SW of the entrance to the Kazikli inlet. The bottom is gently shelving, and shallow at the head and towards the north shore. Anchor in 3–9 m on sand, room for 3 or 4 boats to swing, or a stern line could be run out to a tree to the west.

Caution: Close attention should be paid to the chart for shallow areas west of Kazikli Limani (off Kapali Burun) where shallows extend out some 200 m, and other patches between there and Panayir Adasi. Dangerous to any size of craft is Isabel Kayasi, 1½ miles NW of Kapali Burun, where there is an isolated shoal with a rock only 1 m below the surface.

SAPLI ADASI   37°25'N 27°24'.8E   (No plan)

At the extreme N of the gulf Akbük Limani, this peninsula, Sapli Adasi, provides a fair anchorage on the E side of the isthmus connecting it to the shore.

Approaching up the gulf, one sees what looks like a village at the head, but is in fact a community of summer villas, and Sapli Adasi is low-lying 1 mile to NW of this.

Anchor to the south of the deserted stone building standing just to the east of the root of the isthmus, in 3–4 m on sand, but do not approach anywhere within 100 m of the shore as the bottom here, as in much of the surrounding area, is very gently shelving.

A rather open place, with low-lying land all round except for the ridge of hills to the NE, but affording adequate protection fron NW and N, but only fair from S as there is a 2–4 mile fetch across the gulf.

In winds from W or NW the bay is a paradise for board sailors.

ALTINKUM (Karakuyu Koyu)   37°20'.2N 27°16'.9E   (No plan)

A very hurriedly built seaside holiday town, and still growing at speed, on a magnificent stretch of sandy beach, providing a rather open anchorage, but adequately protected from NW and N. There are numerous restaurants and cafés, and a bakery and shops for essential provisions.

This is the best place from which to visit the temple and quite extensive ruins at Didim, either by minibus or taxi. There are also services from the bus station to major towns in the surrounding area.

Anchor anywhere off the beach in 3–8 m on firm sand, but do not approach within 200 m of the shore as the bottom is very gently shelving. Approaching from SW, keep well offshore in the vicinity of the rocky mole in the SW corner of the bay as shallows extend out around it to E and SE some 500–600 m.

The bay is wide open from SW to SE, and also after a daytime W or NW winds there is often some swell working into the bay from SW after sunset.

ÇUKURCUK LIMAN   37°21'.3N 27°12'.4E   (No plan)

A small bay on a rather uninteresting and featureless low-lying coast, but providing the last shelter from NW and N before leaving the Mandalya gulf.

The mouth of the bay is rather difficult to identify but lies $\frac{2}{3}$ mile E from Tekağaç Burnu lighthouse point.

The arms to NE and W are silted, and one can only anchor immediately inside the mouth in 4 m depth. A stern line to a rock on shore to the NW would be possible.

Open from SW to SE.

CHAPTER 10

Mandalya Gulf to Kuş Adasi

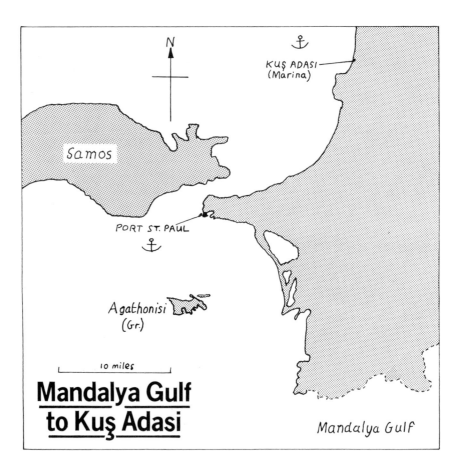

Harbours and anchorages

	Open to:	Comments:
Port St. Paul	SW/S	Poor in strong W'ly winds
Kuş Adasi (marina) Port of entry	–	–

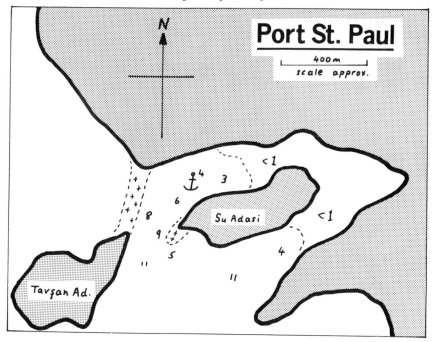

PORT ST. PAUL (Tavşan Adasi)   37°39′.3N 27°00′.7E

The only anchorage on the Turkish coast between Kuş Adasi and the Mandalya Gulf, providing reasonable shelter from NW to NE, but open SW to SE, and partially to W.

Close south of Dipburnu point is the island Tavşan Adasi, with Su Adasi inside it. One cannot enter the anchorage by passing to the N of Tavşan Adasi as there is a bar connecting it to the shore, and also the whole of the inner area to NE of Su Adasi is too shallow to enter. The only suitable area for anchoring therefore is on the north side of Su Adasi, marked on the plan. The anchorage is not recommended at all in unsettled weather, since as well as being poorly protected, winds here can be very strong and variable.

KUŞ ADASI (Marina)   37°52′.2N 27°15′.7E   Port of Entry

This is certainly the best equipped marina in Turkey, with safe mooring for any size of yacht. There is a small harbour in the town nearby, but it is crowded with local fishing boats, and not normally used by yachts. The

Kuş Adasi

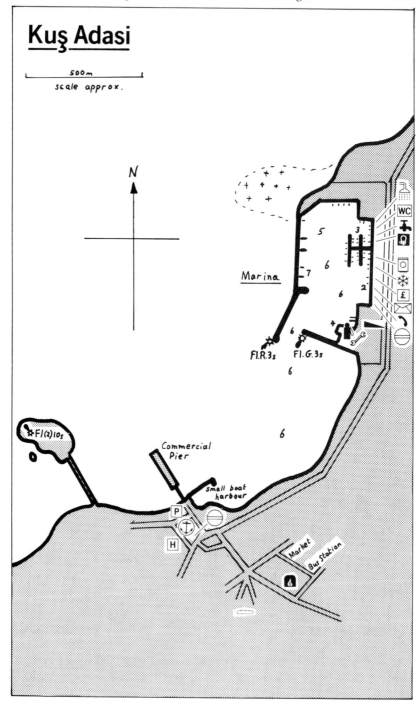

500m
scale approx.

N

5

3

6

7   6

Marina   2

6

6

Fl.R.3s   Fl.G.3s

6

6

☆Fl(2)10s   6

Commercial
Pier

small boat
harbour

P

H

Market   Bus Station

WC

town itself has a growing tourist industry, a number of hotels, and is on the itinerary of a number of cruise ships in the season.

The main attraction is the extensive ruins of the ancient city of Ephesus; well worth a visit, and only a short distance away by bus or taxi.

The marina is always full in the winter, but less crowded in summer when boats move out to the better cruising areas around Bodrum, Marmaris, Fethiye and Rhodes.

The only commonly expressed disadvantage to wintering here is that the marina is rather far from the centre of town. A bicycle or small motor bike is very useful.

Approaching and mooring

Approaching from S, it is best to stay at least one mile offshore until well north of Kuş Adasi town to avoid all of the unmarked shallows lying to W and SW of the town. There is in fact a passage inside both Karakeçi Bank and Yalenci Burnu Bank, but requiring very accurate navigation or local knowledge.

Coming from the Samos Strait, the apparent town one sees is not Kuş Adasi town, but a development of hotels and villas on the shore to the S of the point Yalenci Burnu. Kuş Adasi town and marina do not come into view until you are N of Yalenci Burnu.

In the marina, moor as directed by the berthing master, who may attract your attention with a whistle. All berths are provided with a chain strop to the main ground chain for securing to the bow, taking lines from the stern to the pontoon. Larger yachts on the outer wall often supplement this with their own ground tackle.

Facilities

🍾 ⚓ ❄ £ ⛽ 🔧 ✉ 🎣 ⎯ 🚿 🔌 ⬜

In town: 🔥 ✚ D ✂

Port of entry officials are unfortunately all in the town, but officials for yachts in transit are in the marina.

As with Bodrum marina, one will be charged for a minimum three day period, except if stopping for up to 8 hours during daytime, when one will only be charged for one day. Rates are a little more reasonable than Bodrum, but also priced in dollars so as to be inflation-proof.

Provisions are available in the marina, and there is a bar. Restaurants are in town, or on the road into town.

Showers are much more plentiful than in Bodrum, but again appear to be only solar heated, so there is only limited hot water, and only in fine weather.

Water and electricity points at the berths are plentiful, and charged extra if required. A Travel Hoist (60 tons) and a dry dock are available in the marina.

Buses in town connect with all the inter-city routes, there is a ferry service to Samos (only according to demand out of season), and Izmir airport is only a short distance up the coast.

Bath time for the camels, Mandalya Gulf

Part Three

THE DODECANESE ISLANDS

INTRODUCTION

Lying close of the Turkish coast, the Greek Dodecanese group of islands exhibit just about every possible shade of style and character ranging from those still entirely unspoilt, seldom having any visitors at all, such as Arki, Fourni, and Agathonisi, to the busy popular holiday islands of Samos, Kos and Rhodes.

Most are rocky, mountainous and barren when approached by sea, but conceal, in many cases, safe and delightful anchorages in a number of attractive creeks and inlets, together with usually at least one good harbour, essential for the ferries and cargo carrying boats that provide an island's links with the outside world.

Despite their chequered and at times illustrious history, there are sadly few preserved remains from the ancient civilisations that lived here. The best and most interesting archeological ruins are on Kos, but several of the other islands do have some impressive castles and fortifications worth visiting from the periods of the Byzantines and the crusading knights of St. John; notably Samos, Patmos, Halki and Rhodes.

CHAPTER 11

Samos

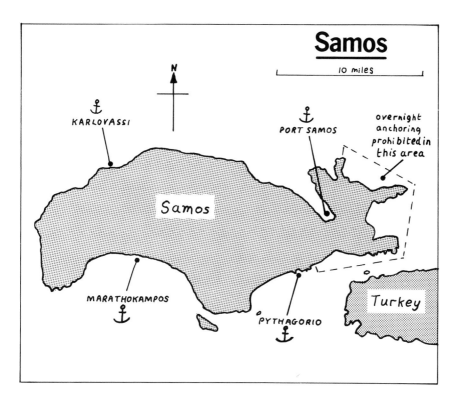

Harbours and anchorages

	Open to:	Comments:
Pythagorio (harbour) Port of Entry	E	Poor in strong S'ly winds
Port Samos (harbour) Port of Entry	N/NW	–
Karlovassi (harbour)	E/NE	–
Marathokampos	SE/S/SW	–

Although strictly not one of the Dodecanese, Samos is included here as it completes the chain of islands likely to be visited by a yacht cruising off this stretch of the Turkish coast.

Although one of the largest islands, it provides rather few interesting ports of call for a yacht, mainly confined to the few harbours of the south coast. This is because it is no longer permitted to moor overnight in the only area well provided with sheltered bays, that is on the east side of the island in the vicinity of the Samos strait, from Pythagorio round to Port Samos.

The island has a small airport catering for domestic flights, as well as international charters in the holiday season.

PYTHAGORIO   37°41′.3N 26°56′.8E   Port of Entry

A typical Greek fishing harbour turned tourist resort, with a number of busy tavernas and cafés lining the harbour front in the season. Behind, there are some attractive and unspoilt parts of the village, with the inhabitants still keeping up their local island way of life.

Approach and mooring
The village is clearly identified approaching from any direction. A small fortress stands close by to the W. Entering the inner harbour, one must keep to north of the red concrete mark to avoid the rocky shallows on the south side.

Moor stern-to the wall to the NW or W of the entrance, but leaving the section of quay painted blue free for local excursion boats.

The harbour front can be a noisy place in the evening, and smelly too as there is a sewage outlet in front of the port captain's office! If seeking a more peaceful spot, one can anchor just outside, to NE of the harbour entrance where there are convenient depths of 4–6 m off the beach.

Protection from all directions except S and SE is good in the harbour, but in W to N winds, gusts can be fierce. In such conditions the anchorage outside is less disturbing. In strong S or SE winds the swell rolls in. Even in NW or N winds some swell can come across from the Samos Strait into the entrance, which can make the place a little uncomfortable for smaller yachts.

Facilities

▲ ⚓ ◨ ❄ £ ◨ ⚲ D ✉ ⌐ ✎ ∞   plus officials for a Port of Entry

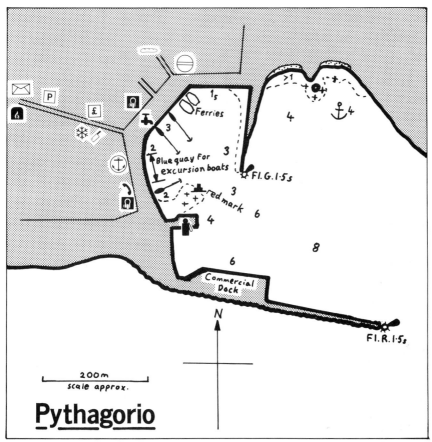

Pythagorio

200m
scale approx.

Enquire at the port office if you wish to take water or fuel at the quay. There is a reluctance to issue only small quantities of fuel from the fuel quay, but there is fuel available at the top of the main street. Greek and Camping gas can be exchanged. The chandler at the S end of the quay can help with water, gas, sail repairs and other requirements.

Scooters, bikes and cars can be hired, and a trip into the interior of the island, more wooded and attractive than most of the Dodecanese, is worth taking.

Ferries run to neighbouring islands, and to Kos, Rhodes, Athens and Kuş Adasi.

PORT SAMOS   37°45′.4N 26°58′.3E   Port of Entry

Although the main town of the island, the harbour is seldom used by yachts as protection from the NW is minimal.

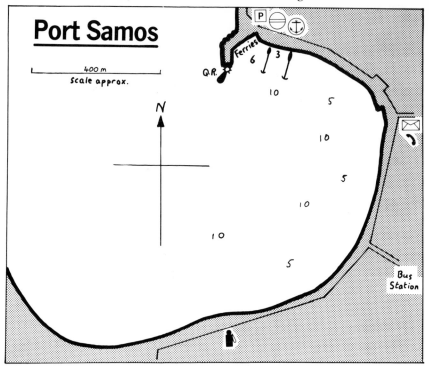

Mooring

There is a very short mole, affording the only protection from the NW, immediately behind which the ferries berth. Moor stern-to as shown on the plan, on the NE wall, and as close to the mole as possible to gain what protection you can from the NW. In southerly winds, the harbour is satisfactory.

Facilities

🔥 £ ✂ ✚ D ✉ ↘ ✎ ⌣ plus Officials for a Port of Entry
Fuel is available by canister in the town. Ferries to most neighbouring islands call here, and to Rhodes and Athens. The telephone office is open 24 hours every day.

KARLOVASSI   37°47′.9N 26°40′.9E

The largest commercial port on the island, not very attractive, and therefore seldom visited by yachts. It is situated on the NW coast.

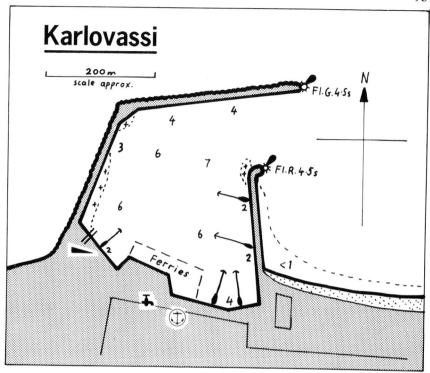

Mooring

Stern-to on the S or E wall, or that part of the wall to the NW not obstructed by shallows, as marked on the plan.

Protection is good from almost all directions, the entrance being open only up the coast to the E. In very strong NW or N winds there is some surge in the harbour, but it is not excessive.

Facilities

There are restaurants and shops for provisions around the harbour area, and also in the town itself a little way along the coast to the E.

A boatyard can haul out quite large motor boats, and shallow draft yachts.

Ferries call here for Ikaria, Leros, and other islands.

MARATHOKAMPOS 37°42′.6N 26°42′E   (No plan)

Situated towards the west on the south coast of the island, this is a charming small fishing village, refreshingly free of tourist development, and providing fair shelter in certain conditions.

Mooring

Two stone piers extend out from the beach, the western one is the longer and acts as a breakwater for the smaller one to the east. The west pier itself is surrounded by water too shallow to enable one to moor up to it.

Moor stern-to, either side of the eastern pier towards its outer end, where depths are 3–4 m.

This anchorage is completely exposed to the southern quadrant, but is adequate with winds from N to NW. In stronger north winds, one should be prepared for some gusts, sometimes quite strong, coming down off the hills behind.

Facilities

There are a few tavernas and cafés, some provisions are available, and a mechanic's workshop.

CHAPTER 12

Fourni

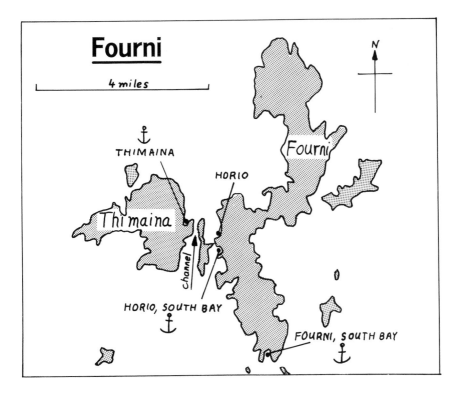

Harbours and anchorages:

	Open to:	Comments:
Horio	N/NW	–
Horio, South bay	S	–
Thimaina	N	–
Fourni, South bay	SE/S/SW	–

This small irregularly shaped island whose main village, Horio, is the only one of any size, together with the neighbouring and even smaller Thimaina island immediately west, provide safe anchorages in any wind direction, and are often used by yachts as a resting point after crossing the Aegean en route to Turkey. The suitable anchorages are all in the vicinity of the narrow channel between the two islands.

The narrow island of Diapori separating Fourni and Thimaina, is almost joined to Fourni, such that the channel from north to south is only to the west of it.

HORIO   37°34'.5N 26°28'.7E   (No plan)

Here, off the main village of the island, anchorage is only possible with winds from the southern quadrant as it is open to the N and NW. The area off the village quay is cluttered with local boats riding at permanent moorings, so if stopping here, perhaps only for a short visit to the village, a trip line on the anchor is advisable, and one should position it with care. The anchorage at South bay (below) is generally much preferred.

Facilities

⚓ ✉ ⌇ ✎ ⌒

There are a few tavernas and cafés, and shops for essential provisions.

A boat runs to Ikaria about once a week.

HORIO – South bay   37°31'.9N 26°30'.5E   (No plan)

To reach here by boat from the main village, Horio, one passes down the channel on the west side of Diapori, around the southern tip, and then proceeds north, almost as far as the point where Diapori nearly touches Fourni. Here there are two beaches on the Fourni shore, and a community of a few small houses.

Anchor off either beach in 6–18 m on weed with patches of clear sand. Open only to the S.

This is a very pleasant spot to spend the night, and only a 20 minute walk over the brow of the headland past the old windmills to the village. To follow the path after dark one definitely needs a torch and a fairly good sense of direction!

There are a couple of tiny cafés on the beach.

THIMAINA   37°34′.9N 26°27′.5E   (No plan)

An alternative anchorage, and better than off Horio village in southerly winds, lies immediately W of the N tip of Diapori, on Thimaina island. There is a village on the slope to the W. Anchor immediately beneath the village, or a little further S into the bay. Do not anchor at the mouth of the bay as there is a cable on the sea-bed. Depths are 4–7 m, sand and light weed.

FOURNI – South bay   37°31′.9N 26°30′.5E   (No plan)

An alternative anchorage in northerly winds, right on the southern tip of Fourni island. An uninhabited barren bay, with rocky shores. Anchor in 5–12 m on sand with room to swing. Open to the southern quadrant.

CHAPTER 13

Agathonisi (Gaidaros)

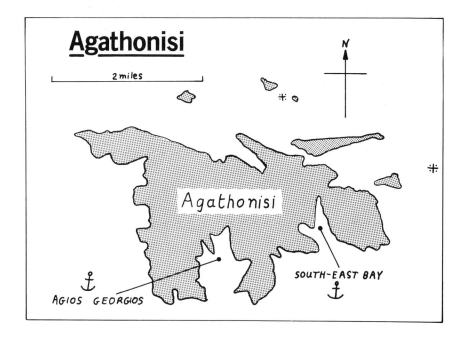

Harbours and anchorages

	Open to:	Comments:
Agios Georgios	SW/S/SE	–
Agathonisi, South-east bay	S/SE	–

Caution: If sailing around Agathonisi, careful attention should be paid to the chart for shoals off the west coast, and close to Strongilo island to the north.

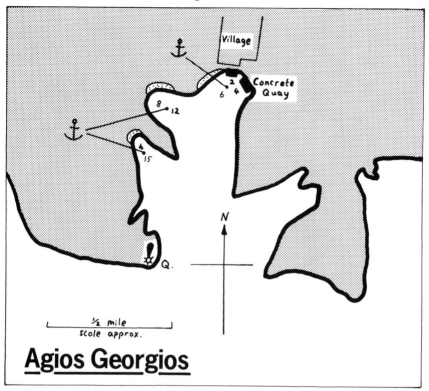

Agios Georgios

AGIOS GEORGIOS   37°27'.2N 26°58'E

An inlet, 1 mile long, on the south coast of the island, with a light on the point to the west side of the mouth, and a small village with a quay at its head.

There is only 1.5 m depth to moor bows-to the small quay in front of the two tavernas at the village, or 8 m stern-to the north side of the concrete commercial wharf just to the right of it. Alternatively, anchor off the village in 4–6 m on a bottom of gently shelving sand.

For a more secluded mooring, anchor as shown on the plan in the NW corner of the inlet in 8–12 m on sand and weed, where a stern line could be run out to a tree on the beach. Or a little S of there where there is a smaller arm projecting, also to NW, with depths of 4–15 m on sand, but with very restricted swinging room.

All of these mooring positions are protected from the northern quadrant, although with strong winds from the high ground to the north, conditions can be gusty. There is no protection here from S.

AGATHONISI – South-east bay   37°27′.5N 26°59′.5E   (No plan)

This inlet on the SE side of the island has two arms, one to the N and one to the W. The better anchorage is in the northern arm which is long, narrow, and very secluded, with a small beach at its head where the width is only some 30 m. Anchor in 2–5 m, with a line to a rock on either side, or both, to prevent swinging into either. Narrowly open to S.

CHAPTER 14

Arki

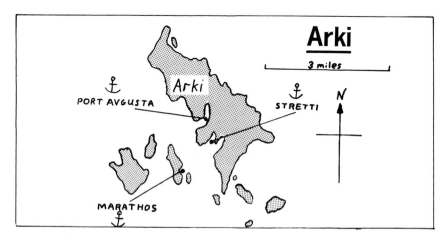

Harbours and anchorages

	Open to:	Comments:
Port Avgusta	–	Less protection from SW for yachts drawing more than 2 m
Port Stretti	SW/S	–
Marathos	S/SE	–

PORT AVGUSTA   37°22′.8N 26°44′E   (No plan)

A delightful narrow little inlet almost half-way up the west coast of the island, with a tiny village community at its head, the only habitation visible on the island. There is a light on the north point at the mouth of the inlet, and soon after you enter there is a bend to the left, and the depths become rather shallow approaching the hamlet. For craft drawing around 2 m or less, able to anchor beyond the bend, there is all round shelter. At the very

Port Avgusta, Arki

head, off the hamlet, the bottom shallows to less than 1.5 m. There is not room to swing, so one should anchor by the bow and stern, or take lines ashore. The bottom is sand.

Yachts drawing more than 2.5 m should not proceed beyond the bend, but should anchor there where the depth is around 10 m. Partially open to W and S.

There is one taverna in the village, and some provisions may be available.

PORT STRETTI   37°22′.5N 26°44′.3E   (No plan)

The next inlet immediately south of Port Avgusta, divided into two parts by a narrow peninsula. In the southern part, anchor in 10–17 m on weed and sand with room to swing. Uninhabited.

The northern arm is much longer, with a white chapel with a domed roof at its head, but beyond the beach on the right hand side half-way into the inlet, depths are less than 1.5 m. Before reaching this point one can anchor in 3–8 m, preferably with a line ashore as there is little room to swing.

Both arms are open to some swell from S to SW, but protected from all other directions.

MARATHOS   37°22'.1N 26°43'.7E   (No plan)

This small island just off the entrance to Stretti and Port Avgusta has an anchorage on its E side, to the NW of an even smaller nameless off-lying islet. A small villa and a cottage are on the shore. Note that the channel between the small islet and Marathos, if approached from S, is obstructed by a shallow area in the centre. Anchoring depths in the cove are 8–15 m, on coarse sand with weed and some stones. Open only to swell from S or SE, otherwise quite well protected.

CHAPTER 15

Lipsos

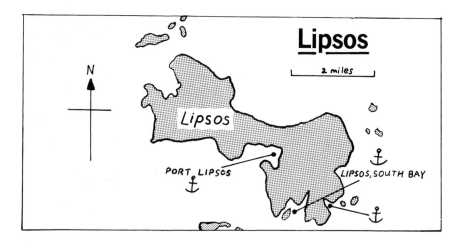

Harbours and anchorages

	Open to:	Comments:
Port Lipsos (harbour)	–	Anchorage close by better in strong SW winds
Lipsos, South bay	SW/S/SE	–

PORT LIPSOS   37°17'.6N 26°45'.7E

Not a very attractive harbour, but a pleasant and unspoilt village, the main one of the island.

Mooring
Approaching from west the village and quay are clearly visible at the head of the inlet. Moor bows-to in any of the positions marked on the plan. Depths are limited as indicated.

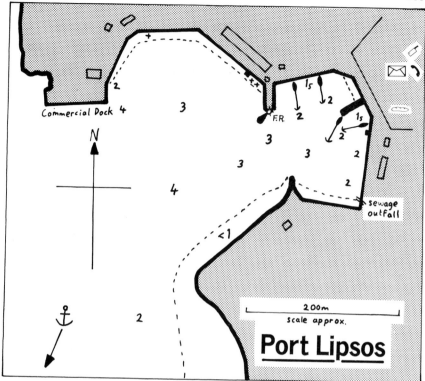

Port Lipsos

200m
scale approx.

The harbour is well protected except from W and SW. If it should become uncomfortable, one could go instead alongside the E end of the commercial dock where depths are 3 m or more.

There is also room to anchor off the village and swing, or one could anchor in the well protected cove to the south in 2–6 m on weed on mud, but do not proceed more than half-way into this cove as it becomes very shallow some way out from the shore.

Facilities

☒ ⸜ ⸝ ⸜⸝

There are a few tavernas and cafés around the harbour and in the village. Boats run infrequently to Patmos and Leros according to demand.

LIPSOS – South bay   37°16′.8N 26°46′.5E   (No plan)

This bay, immediately west of the extreme southern tip of Lipsos, contains an islet occupying a large part of its W side.

Entering up the channel to the W side of this islet, and just before coming abreast of its northern tip, one can anchor in 4–7 m on sand with some weed. Beyond, further in to the north, is anchorage in similar depths, where there are a few houses and a chapel.

Alternatively, enter to the east of the islet, and proceed up the narrow inlet to the north of here, where, about half-way in one can anchor in 3–6 m, but the bottom is very gently shelving, and most yachts will not be able to go any further in than this point. The only building in sight, visible at the head of the inlet, is a small church.

The channel to the north of the islet has a maximum depth of about 4 m.

All parts of this bay are open in some degree to swell from the southern quadrant.

Anchorage is also reasonably good in the bay immediately E of the southern tip of Lipsos, in depths of 6–12 m, where protection from SW is slightly better. But the bay is otherwise wide open to the SE quadrant.

Caution: Sailing around SE Lipsos note that a shoal with only about 2 m depth over it extends out more than a mile from the shore.

CHAPTER 16

Patmos

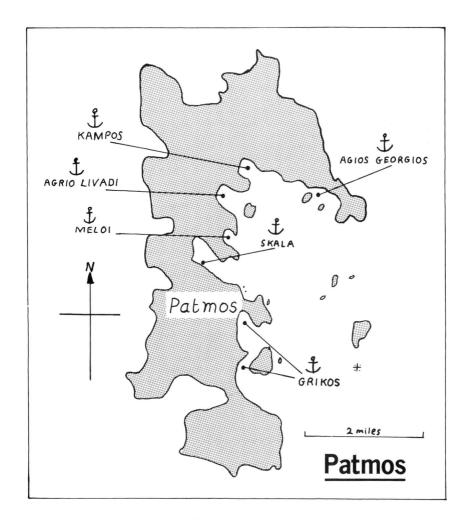

KAMPOS

AGRIO LIVADI

MELOI

AGIOS GEORGIOS

SKALA

N

Patmos

GRIKOS

2 miles

Patmos

Harbours and anchorages

	Open to:	Comments:
Skala	E/SE	Anchorage close by gives even better protection
Meloi	E/SE/S	–
Agrio Livadi	E/SE/S	–
Kampos	SE/S	–
Agios Georgios	SE/S	–
Grikos	SE/E	More protection from SE possible behind islet

An increasingly popular holiday island, but as yet, relatively unspoilt. The fortified monastery of St. John is an impressive sight, standing on the summit of the hill south of the main port, Skala, with the white painted houses of the principal town, Hora, huddled on the slopes around it. From Skala, Hora and the monastery are within walking distance. The east coast of the island forms a large bay, around which the other anchorages mentioned are situated. This whole area is well protected from generally W and NW summer winds, and is ideal for board sailing, water-skiing and the like.

SKALA   37°19′.4N 26°32′.8E

Not a very inspiring harbour, but with an unspoilt and well kept village of dazzling white Cycladian style houses. The main port of the island.

Mooring
Stern-to immediately to the left after passing the ferry quay. An unlit buoy lies about 100 m off the yacht quay.

There is not room here for many yachts, but there is alternative mooring at the anchorage right at the head of the inlet in 3–8 m on mud and weed.

Only a SW swell causes any discomfort, and in such conditions the best place to be is anchored as tight in to the extreme NE as possible, right at the head of the inlet, off the fuel jetty.

Facilities

There are a number of restaurants, tavernas and cafés, and shops for all provisions.

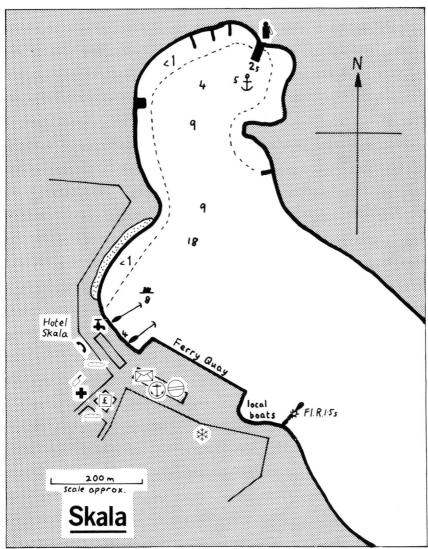

Skala

Water is from a hose on the quay, but is reported to be often less than crystal-clear. If the attendant is not there to turn it on, ask at the Hotel Skala. The fuel on the jetty at the head of the inlet is in drums, but can be piped straight to a yacht.

Mopeds and motor bikes are available for hire.

Ferries run to most islands round about, and to Rhodes and Athens two or three times a week in the season. There are also hydrofoils to Kos and Rhodes regularly in summer.

MELOI   37°19′.8N 26°33′.4E   (No plan)

The first of several anchorages to the north of Skala, this is in the bay immediately N of the lit point to the NE of Skala harbour.

There are two tavernas on the beach at the head of the bay, and a camping ground.

The sea-bed is more steeply shelving than the other anchorages further north, with depths of 7–15 m on weed and sand but with some stony areas. Room to swing. Open to SE.

AGRIO LIVADI   37°20′.4N 26°33′.5E   (No plan)

The next bay north of Meloi, with an islet partially blocking the mouth. Enter to the north of the islet and keep to the north, towards the Patmos shore, as there are rocks to be avoided off the islet.

There are only a few buildings on shore, in a grove of trees on the beach.

The bottom is gently shelving, with depths of 4–9 m, sand and weed, over a good size area for anchoring. Open only partially to SE past the islet at the mouth.

KAMPOS   37°20′.9N 26°34′E   (No plan)

Lying immediately north of Agrio Livadi, this is the northernmost bay on this part of the shore. One taverna and a board sailing school are on the beach at the head. At the left hand end of the beach a road leads to a small village.

Again, a large anchoring area, on a gently shelving bottom of sand and weed, with depths of 4–7 m. Similarly well protected to the other bays between here and Skala, being open only to the SE.

AGIOS GEORGIOS   37°20′.6N 26°35′.3E   (No plan)

Approximately 1 mile ESE of Kampos is the islet Agios Georgios, with anchorage off the beach on the Patmos shore immediately NNE of it. This is a more secluded spot for those seeking somewhere away from the tourist beaches.

Entrance to the anchorage is best from the south, passing between

Agios Georgios islet and the smaller islet just to the east of it. The channels between both of the islets and the shore are shallow and rocky.

There are a few buildings on the beach in a grove of trees, but they appear normally uninhabited.

Anchor off the beach in 3–7 m on sand. Quite good protection from most directions, but open to the south.

GRIKOS   37°18′N 26°33′.8E   (No plan)

Two miles SSE of Skala lies Grikos Bay, with the off-lying islet Traonisi. Grikos village is in the NW corner of the bay, with a few small hotels and tavernas. Anchor off the village in 7–12 m or, for a quieter anchorage, move further to the S, and anchor off the beach W of Traonisi islet. Both anchorages are partially open to E and S, but in the event of a SE'ly swell, some protection can be gained by anchoring close up behind Traonisi islet, on its NW side, off a small beach immediately to the S of a tiny white cottage. Here the bottom is sand and weed, and depths are 6–12 m.

The large square rock standing strangely isolated on the beach with several cave-like shelters cut into it, was apparently home for a small community of hippies in the 1960s.

CHAPTER 17

Leros

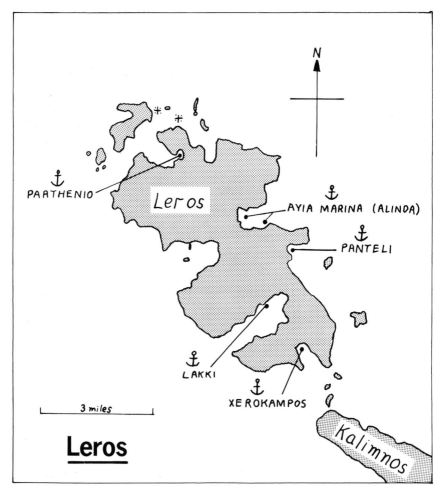

Leros

Caution: Approaching Parthenio at the northern end of the island from E or NE, note the shallows off the extreme northern tip of the island, and close to the east side of Archangelos island which lies off to the NW.

Harbours and anchorages

	Open to:	Comments:
Lakki (harbour)	–	Chop comes from across the bay in strong S/SE'ly winds
Parthenio	–	–
Ayia Marina (Alinda)	NE/E/SE	–
Panteli	E/SE	–
Xerokampos	S/SE	Some rebound swell in SW'ly winds

A rather odd mixture of declining naval activity, traditional island life, and tourism development in its early stages will be found on different parts of the island. Nevertheless, there are one or two very pleasant anchorages, and the main village Platanos, up on a hill on the E coast with a fine castle above it on a headland, has considerable charm. It can be reached by foot from Agia Marina or Panteli.

A small propeller plane operates an occasional service to Kos, Rhodes and Athens, mainly in summer from an airstrip at the north of the island.

LAKKI   37°07'.6N 26°51'E

This is the largest port on Leros, but is now somewhat in decline. In past years it had some importance as a naval base, but all that remains now is a small naval establishment on the S shore a short distance inside the entrance. One should keep well away from this area, as approaching it is likely to arouse suspicion.

Lakki is not in any way an attractive harbour, and is not worth a special visit.

Approach and mooring

Approaching from SW, steep rocks and a light on both sides of the mouth, quite easily identify the entrance. The yacht quay is tucked around to the left almost at the head of the inlet, just before reaching the town, also on the left hand shore.

A lit buoy, shown on the plan, lies close off the mooring area. Go stern-to the wall to the west, but with care, as it is in a poor state of repair with cracked concrete and reinforcing rods exposed. There are few proper attachment points for lines. Beware, rats have been seen on the quay here!

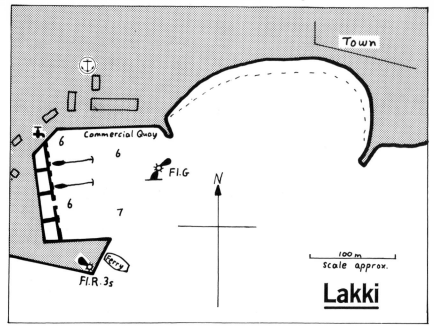

Lakki

Protection is practically all round. Only a southerly blow will cause an uncomfortable chop for smaller yachts.

Facilities

Water is on the quay, but fuel can only be collected by canister from the town.

Mopeds and motorbikes can be hired.

Ferries to most neighbouring islands as well as to Athens and Rhodes call here.

PARTHENIO　37°11′.4N 26°48′.5E　(No plan)

This inlet lies to the NW of the island, with its mouth protected from the NW by the off-lying Archangelos island. Avoid some large naval buoys at the mouth of the inlet on the west side. There is a tiny airport runway at the head. But neither of these are usually any nuisance, the buoys being very seldom used and some way from the anchorage, and the airstrip having seldom as much as one plane a day.

The anchorage itself is in a landlocked basin around to the left just before the head of the inlet. Entering the basin, the depth is 10 m, shelving gently up to the shore, and shallow close in. Anchor anywhere in the bay on a bottom of weed and mud.

A tiny community of only a couple of houses on the SE side is the only sign of habitation. This is invariably a quiet and peaceful anchorage, and provides all round protection.

AYIA MARINA (Alinda)   37°09'.7N 26°50'.5E   (No plan)

Alinda bay is the large bay immediately N of the castle on the E coast of the island. The village of Ayia Marina is on the S side at the mouth of the bay, beneath both the castle and the main village of the island, Platanos, which is only a short walk up the hill. This is the growing holiday area of the island, with several hotels springing up around the perimeter of the bay, but it is still in the very early stages of development.

Mooring
Normally it is best to anchor off the W shore of the bay where there are depths of 5–10 m on a gently shelving bottom of sand and weed. Well protected from almost all directions, but open to E.

The village quay is not very suitable for yachts, with poor holding on a stony bottom, and too shallow for most yachts even to go bows-to. However the projecting portion of the quay, used by ferries and caiques unloading goods has 3–4 m alongside, and one can stop here for limited periods if not interfering with commercial traffic.

Facilities

In the village: £ ✚ ✉ ⌐ ⌒ ⚲

There are tavernas in the village, and also around the perimeter of the bay. Provisions are available in Ayia Marina, or up the hill in Platanos.

Some of the ferries to nearby islands call in here.

PANTELI   37°09'N 26°51'.8E   (No plan)

Immediately to the south of the headland on which stands the castle and the village of Platanos, Panteli bay provides a good summer anchorage, well protected from W and NW although widely open to the SE.

There are a few tavernas on the beach at the head of the bay, and Platanos village and the castle are only a short walk up the hill.

Anchor off the beach in 4–12 m on sand and light weed, with room to swing. The short mole is too shallow for yachts. For a quieter spot, anchor off the beach close by to the SW where there are only a couple of buildings on the shore. Here depths are 4–8 m, also on sand and light weed.

XEROKAMPOS   37°06'.4N 26°52'.3E   (No plan)

This large inlet on the S coast of Leros provides fairly good anchorage in rather uninteresting surroundings. One restaurant stands on the beach at the head of the inlet, with a small village of concrete houses just beyond.

The bottom is very gently shelving, with convenient depths of 4–12 m over a large area. Holding is on sand and weed.

Swell running along the S coast of the island from the W in a W or NW wind will work into the inlet. For a small yacht it can become uncomfortable. Open to SE.

CHAPTER 18

Kalimnos

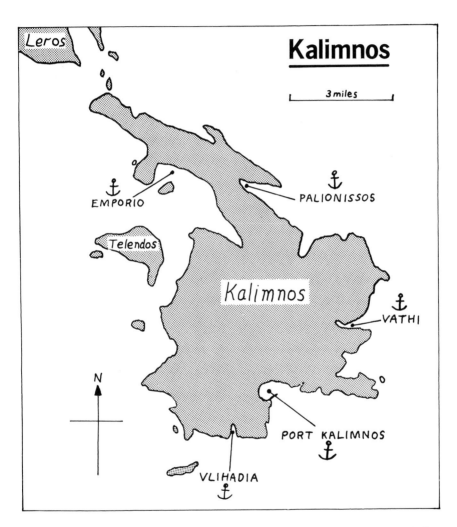

Caution: If passing between the northern tip of Kalimnos and the closest off-lying island, Glaronisia, keep to the Kalimnos side as there are shallows off the island.

Harbours and anchorages

	Open to:	Comments:
Port Kalimnos (harbour)	E/SE	Rebound swell in strong S'ly winds
Vathi	E	All round protection for yachts less than 2 m draught
Palionissos	E/SE/S	Plus some rebound swell in strong N'ly winds
Emporio (Borio)	SE/S/SW	Islet affords limited protection from south
Vlihadia	SE/S/SW	–

Most of the population of Kalimnos are in the large busy town at the main port. All the other villages and hamlets on the island are comparatively small, with some limited tourist hotel development on the west coast near Telendos island, on some rather poor beaches.

For a visiting yacht however, the island does have a few very pleasant coves in which to spend the night.

PORT KALIMNOS   36°56′.9N 26°59′.3E

A large harbour, and a busy town, being the modern capital of the island, Kalimnos has long been a centre for sponge fishermen. Although the trade is now in decline there are still some divers regularly employed, and their wares are displayed for sale all around town.

Numerous cafés and tavernas line the harbour front serving the large numbers of tourists in the season, but there are also some quieter more unspoilt areas to be found in the labyrinth of back streets.

Mooring

The harbour is protected by a substantial concrete dock extending NE from the SW side. The yacht quay is at the root of this where one moors stern-to, but space is rather limited. The SW wall close by is normally reserved for commercial craft, but if the yacht quay is full one may be able to find space here.

Protection is good from all directions, but in strong southerly winds a swell rebounds around the harbour, and in very strong north-westerlies

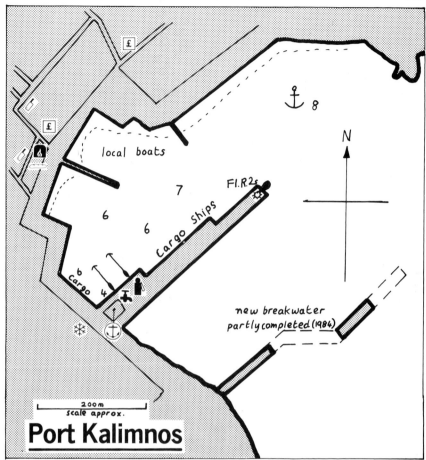

Port Kalimnos

the chop set up in the harbour can be uncomfortable for small craft. In such conditions it may be preferred to anchor in the NNE part of the harbour where gusts are less severe and there is space for several yachts to swing.

Inside this harbour, and all along the S coast of Kalimnos, NW winds are always gusty and stronger than further offshore in open water.

A new outer breakwater, its approximate position marked on the plan, should be completed during 1985.

Facilities

Water is provided by hose on the yacht quay. Diesel fuel is also on the quay, but there can be some difficulty finding anyone in attendance. Enquire at the Port Captain's office.

If any difficulties are experienced in obtaining supplies or finding repair or other facilities, the brothers at the restaurant behind the port office have always been most helpful to visiting yachtsmen.

Ferry services run from here to most other surrounding islands, and to Rhodes and Athens.

Scooters and motorbikes are available for hire, and it is an enjoyable ride through the villages in the interior of the island and up the west coast to Emporio.

VATHI   36°58′.4N 27°02′.3E

Lying just over a mile north of the SE tip of Kalimnos, this very narrow inlet has a quite remarkable entrance with sheer rock cliffs towering on both sides. The inlet quickly becomes very narrow, and bends to the right to reveal the small village at the head. Only the smallest yachts drawing around 1.5 m should proceed beyond the bend since it becomes shallower and manoeuvring room is very restricted, although shelter is more complete.

On the left hand side at the bend is a short projecting jetty with space

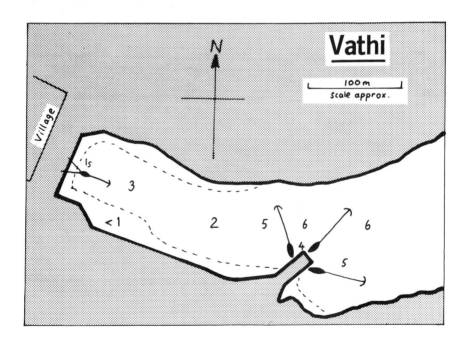

Vathi, Kalimnos

for four or five yachts to moor stern-to. Yachts with shallow draft may find space to moor bows-to the quay right at the head of the inlet in front of the village, but even then will probably not be able to get close enough to step ashore as it becomes very shallow close up to the wall.

There are a couple of tavernas and two tiny shops for basic provisions. A bus runs occasionally to Kalimnos town.

Although W and NW winds funnel strongly down the inlet, it is well protected from swell from all directions except E.

PALIONISSOS   37°02′.3N 26°58′.4E   (No plan)

A rugged and isolated inlet on the east coast, approximately six miles SE from the northern tip of the island, offering a wild but secluded anchorage in fair weather. It is over a mile from the mouth at Akra Punta point to the head of the inlet, where there are a couple of apparently uninhabited buildings in the trees just behind the stony beach.

Anchor in 5–17 m on a rather poor bottom of sand and stones. The bay is only open to the SE, but because of the high ground to the west there can be disturbing gusts with winds in the NW quadrant. The anchorage is not therefore recommended except in settled conditions.

EMPORIO (Borio)   37°02′.5N 26°55′.6E   (No plan)

A very pleasant, quiet and peaceful anchorage on the west side of the island, approximately 2 miles NE of Telendos island.

Anchor either off the tiny hamlet at the far north of the bay, where there are depths of 5–12 m on a bottom of sand and weed with some stones and rocks, or for better holding, anchor off the beach close by to the west. Here one can find areas of sand, with some weed, but clear of stones.

Protection is good, except from between SE and SW.

In summer, the hamlet sports one very simple taverna.

VLIHADIA   36°55′.8N 26°58′.1E   (No plan)

A tiny, very quiet and pleasant creek, on the S coast of the island, to the west of Port Kalimnos, a mile beyond cape Agios Georgios.

There are only a few buildings on the beach at the head of the creek, including a small taverna.

Anchor in 4–6 m on sand, with some stones which can make the holding rather insecure. There is room for a medium sized yacht to swing.

The bay is well protected, being only open to S. In strong W to N winds the gusts are much less severe here than in Kalimnos town.

CHAPTER 19

Pserimos

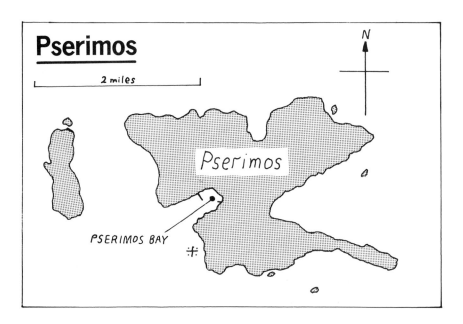

Harbours and anchorages

	Open to:	Comments:
Pserimos Bay (harbour)	W/SW/S	Some limited protection from W/SW behind breakwater

Pserimos is a tiny island, a few miles east of the SE tip of Kalimnos, supporting a small community living mostly around the rather poor harbour at the head of the inlet on the west coast.

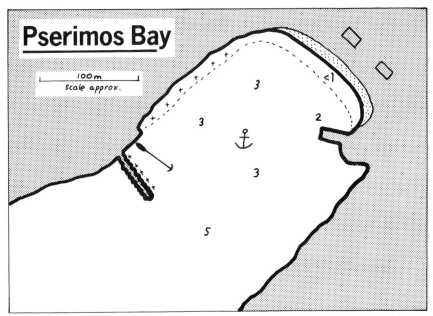

PSERIMOS BAY   36°55′.9N 27°07′.9E

A charming little village with a couple of tavernas stands at the head of the inlet, with a beautiful sand beach which in the season is unfortunately popular with day trippers from nearby Kalimnos.

With only the short breakwater extending out from the north side of the inlet, protection in the harbour is only fair. Stern-to behind the breakwater is the best position, if there is space, or simply anchor and swing. You can moor to the jetty at the right hand end of the beach, but will have to move off it before the excursion boats start arriving during the season at about ten o'clock in the morning.

Open to the SW; any wind from S to NW will cause some swell to enter. There is even some disturbance with a strong N wind.

Caution: Between the mouth of Pserimos Bay and Cape Sphiri (the SW tip of Pserimos island) one should keep well out from the coast as there are rocky shallows spreading out nearly 400 m from the shore.

CHAPTER 20

Kos

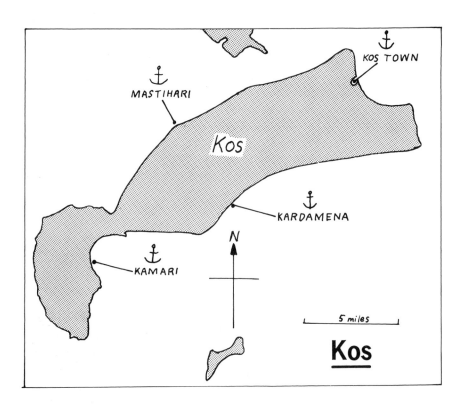

Harbours and anchorages

	Open to:	Comments:
Kos Town (harbour) Port of Entry	N/NE	–
Mastihari	E/NE	Uncomfortable in strong N/NW winds
Kamari	E/SE	Poor in S'ly winds
Kardamena (harbour)	E	Depth limited to 2 m

Despite the popular present day image of Kos as a fast-growing beach holiday resort centre, it has a distinguished ancient history. The island contains some of the best-preserved and restored remains of Classical and Hellenistic civilisations to be seen in the Aegean, although unfortunately many interesting artefacts have been removed to cities on the mainland for exhibition and safekeeping.

Most of the modern tourist trade is centred around the main town and the beaches just to the north of the harbour, but with one other fast growing resort village at Kardamena half-way along the south coast.

The island's airport caters for domestic as well as international charter flights, which partly explains the large number of visitors and the rapid rate of development of the last few years.

The coastline itself is rather disappointing, being devoid of any suitable inlets for anchoring, although there are a few other points apart from the main harbour where breakwaters give satisfactory protection for over-night mooring.

As with Samos and Kalimnos, the south coast of the island rises steeply from the shore to a considerable height, particularly the eastern part, and in N or NW summer winds the strength of the gusts close inshore can be quite alarming. If sailing along the south coast in such conditions, it is advisable to keep at least five miles out.

The site of Asclepius, Kos

KOS TOWN   36°53'.8N 27°17'.3E   Port of Entry

A busy holiday town in the season, with tavernas and cafés jostling for position and vying for trade on the harbour-front. This is also the base for a number of excursion boats, producing a flurry of activity as they depart in the morning, and again when they return in the early evening.

A fine sandy beach stretches away to the north, but naturally it becomes rather crowded in the high season.

Approach and mooring

The narrow entrance to the harbour lies immediately north of the impressive restored castle, built originally by the knights of St John.

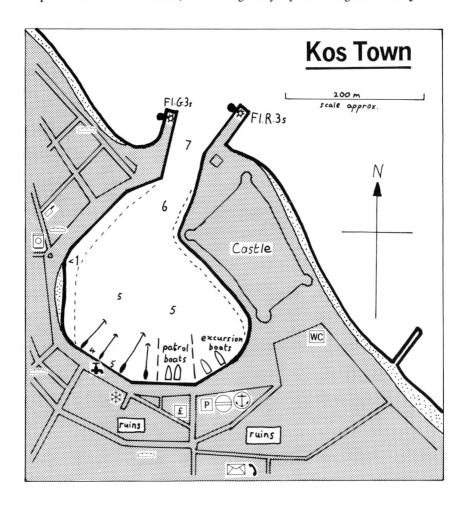

Visiting yachts should moor stern-to on the SW wall opposite the entrance.

The harbour is quite safe in most conditions, but since the entrance is unfortunately open to N, summer winds in the NW often create a swell that runs down the coast from Akra Ammoglossa point and causes quite a disturbance in the harbour, making it somewhat uncomfortable for smaller yachts. A sewage outfall in the southern corner, just to the right of the port office, can be rather unpleasant if moored too close to it.

Facilities

⚓ ❄ £ 🔧 ✚ ✉ ⌐ ⌐ ⊘ ▣ plus officials for a Port of Entry.

The fuel station is some way from the harbour, but if taking on a fair quantity, a bowser can deliver to the quay.

Motorbikes or cars can be hired to visit the archaeological sites and the interior of the island.

As well as the airport, serving Rhodes, Athens, and occasionally some other islands, there are many ferry services calling here both to the surrounding islands, and to Rhodes, Athens, and the Cyclades. Also a hydrofoil runs daily in the season to Rhodes.

MASTIHARI   36°51'.1N 27°04'.7E   (No plan)

This is the only protection on the north coast of the island, provided by an L-shaped rock breakwater extending N and then E. This creates a harbour which is open to the E up the coast. A small village of no special interest stands next to it.

Approach and mooring

Situated about half-way along the N coast of the island, the village and the quite substantial rock breakwaters are fairly easily identifiable from seaward. Enter around the E end of the outer wall, and moor stern-to or alongside any part of either breakwater in 3–4 m, bearing in mind that the provision of rings and bollards is rather poor.

The harbour is not as well protected from NW'ly swell as it might appear, with often some disturbance inside the breakwaters, becoming worse if the wind moves further N or NE.

Facilities

A couple of tavernas, a few shops for limited provisions, and a baker.
A boat to Kalimnos runs regularly in summer.

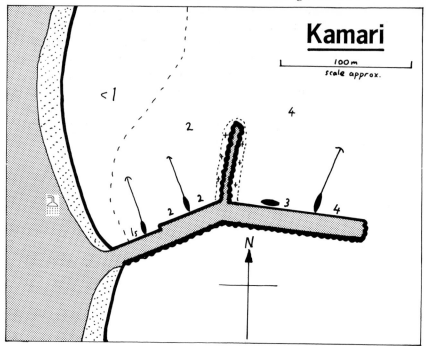

KAMARI   36°44′.3N 26°58′.5E

Here is fairly good protection beside a concrete jetty in the bay towards the western end of the south coast of the island, just where the shoreline turns southwards.

Although the range of hills to the NW are quite high, the gusts created in NW winds are not generally too severe. Protection is normally quite adequate, except from the E and SE, when even the short breakwater projecting out from the jetty is only partially effective in sheltering small craft able to find space amongst the fishing boats to moor inside it.

In high summer when southerly winds are unlikely to occur anchorage off the beach to the NE is satisfactory.

There are a few tavernas nearby, and cold showers on the beach.

KARDAMENA   36°46′.6N 27°08′.6E   (No plan)

A busy small resort village in the season, with a beautiful sandy beach stretching some distance away to the west.

The very shallow harbour, formed by an L-shaped rock breakwater, is largely silted with sand, and is only suitable for small yachts, the maximum depth being only 2 m. The deepest part is at the end of a concrete jetty that extends out from the shore side into the centre of the harbour, and this is the only spot where it is possible to go bows-to. Usually a cluster of local boats at this point means it can be difficult to nudge in between them.

The harbour is open only out through the entrance to NE. Shelter from other directions is good. Gusts from NW off the island are not too severe. Care is needed to enter in SE'ly winds, and if these are strong a big swell would make the approach impossible.

Facilities

There are a number of restaurants, bars and cafés in the village, and motorbikes and cars can be hired to explore the island and visit the archeological sites.

CHAPTER 21

Nissiros

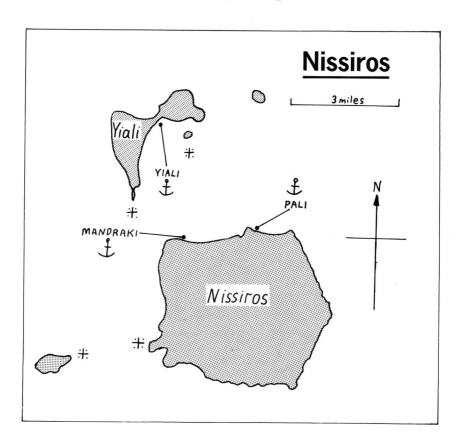

Harbours and anchorages

	Open to:	Comments:
Mandraki (harbour)	NE/E	Poor in strong N/NW winds
Pali (harbour)	N	Entrance difficult in strong NW/N/NE winds
Yiali	S/SE/E	–

Caution: Approaching from the west between Yiali and Nissiros keep well clear of the rocks awash off the south tip of Yiali.

Although the harbours of Nissiros are of a rather poor standard, together with the anchorage on the S side of the island of Yiali just to the N, one can find protection here from winds from any direction.

Nissiros is well worth a visit, not only for its delightful and totally unspoilt villages, but also for the trip to the volcano crater in the interior of the island, reached by bus from Mandraki. If one takes the trouble to walk down into the crater itself there are fascinating bubbling pools and a gushing steam at the bottom.

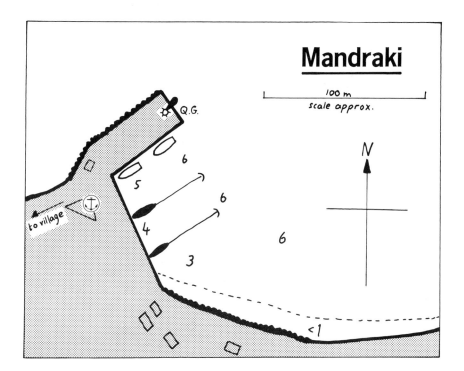

MANDRAKI   36°37′N 27°08′.5E

A rather poor harbour formed by only one short breakwater extending NE. The village close by to the west has considerable charm, and it is from here that one can take the bus to visit the volcano crater. The timetable for departures coincides with the arrival of boats or hydrofoils running excursions from Kos and Rhodes.

Mooring

The harbour is immediately E of the village, which is clearly visible from seaward. Approach around the E end of the breakwater, and moor stern-to the W wall. One may be able to lie alongside the breakwater, but only after the last excursion boats have left in the late afternoon.

The harbour is wide open to NE, and with NW winds some swell will invariably occur, becoming worse as the wind moves more northerly.

Facilities

A few restaurants and cafés as well as shops for most provisions, including a butcher, are in the village.

PALI   36°37′.3N 27°10′.4E

Another pretty and unspoilt village, with a harbour formed by rough stone breakwaters providing fair protection.

A conspicuous white chapel stands on a headland immediately W of the harbour. As shown on the plan, the entrance between the two breakwaters is very narrow, and further restricted by underwater rocks just off the end

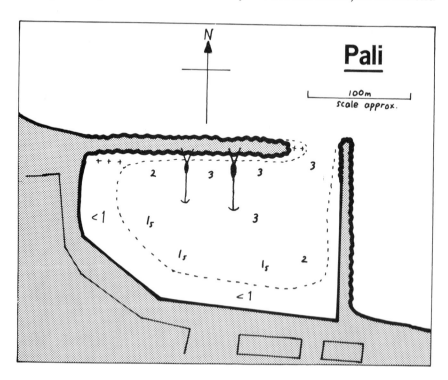

of the N breakwater. With a sizeable swell from anywhere in the northern quadrant it is not recommended to attempt this entrance.

Mooring bows-to the north breakwater, it is possible in some parts to approach close enough to step ashore, but the foundations are uneven and one should approach with care. All other parts of the perimeter of the harbour are silted and too shallow for most yachts.

Since the entrance is open to N, any swell from the northern quadrant will cause a disturbance in the harbour. But as long as winds are not strong it is not unduly uncomfortable. Protection from SW to SE is good.

There are a few tavernas and cafés, as well as limited provisions and a baker in the village.

YIALI   36°39'.8N 27°07'.7E   (No plan)

In strong NE to NW winds, when both harbours on Nissiros become unsuitable, there is safe anchorage on the S side of Yiali island, 3 miles NNW of Nissiros protected by the isthmus joining the hills at either end of the island.

The islet Agios Andonis, close to the SE of Yiali, has underwater as well as visible rocks just S of it, and one should keep well clear if approaching from the NE before turning north to the anchorage.

Immediately to the W of the isthmus is a quarry, clearly visible, and a loading jetty for ships. Indeed there are often ships anchored off waiting to load.

Anchor off the sandy shore of the isthmus on a gently sloping sandy bottom, with depths of 3–6 m.

Well protected from NE to W, but wide open SE to SW.

CHAPTER 22

Tilos

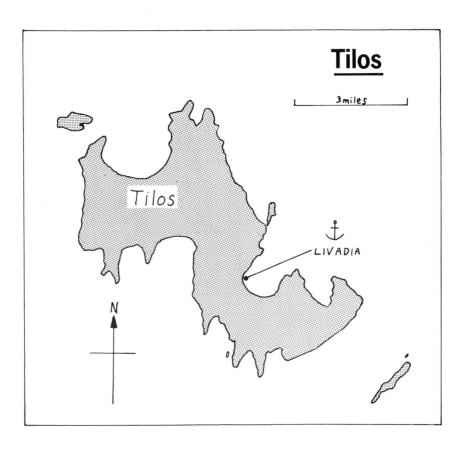

Harbours and anchorages

	Open to:	*Comments*:
Livadia (quay)	E/NE	Poor in N/NW'ly winds

Tilos is not worth a special visit in a yacht, having only a very poor harbour at the unspoilt but uninteresting village of Livadia on the E side of the island.

LIVADIA   36°25′.1N 27°23′.3E

Situated to the NW at the head of a large bay on the E side of the island, the only provision here for mooring is a concrete quay to which one can tie alongside. There is no breakwater to offer any protection from the swell from a NW to N wind, which unfortunately runs down the east coast of the island and, only partially diminished, turns and runs SW down to the village and the quay. In summer, this is seldom therefore a comfortable place to spend the night. With winds in the S or SW it is satisfactory, but in a SE'ly, again a swell will run in.

Facilities

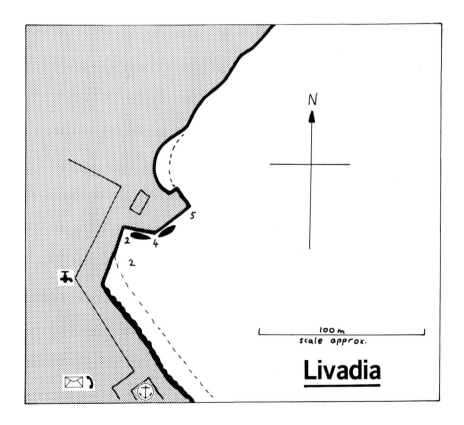

One or two tavernas in summer, and a few cafés are in the village. A few shops provide limited provisions.

Caution: In moderate to strong NW winds there are severe gusts off the N side of the mouth of the bay approaching Livadia quay.

CHAPTER 23

Symi

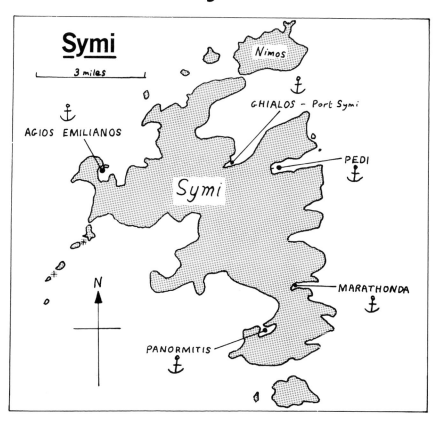

Harbours and anchorages

	Open to:	*Comments:*
Ghialos (Port Symi, harbour)	NE/E	Some disturbance in very strong N/NW winds
Panormitis	–	–
Pedi	E	–
Marathonda	E/SE	Poor in S'ly or NE winds
Agios Emilianos	N/NE	Poor in strong NW winds

Symi is a barren, mountainous island that now makes a large part of its income from tourism. Being one of the closest islands to Rhodes, a number of day-trip boats call here during the summer season.

There are ferry connections to all the other islands of the Dodecanese, and to Athens.

GHIALOS   36°37′N 27°50′.5E

Sometimes referred to as Port Symi, this is the main harbour of the island. The attractive, brightly-painted houses spread up to the hillside to the capital, Horio, which is reached by steps from the SW corner of the harbour. The view from the top, after about a twenty minute climb, is superb.

Although not a Port of Entry, it is possible to sail from here to Turkey by clearing customs in Rhodes, and stopping off 'in transit'.

Mooring
Stern-to on the W quay. Holding is fairly good, although the bottom is rather firm and stony in places. When that is full, yachts can use the western half of the N wall, but off most of this the bottom is too deep to anchor stern-to, so one may have to go alongside. The eastern half of this wall is used by excursion boats.

If the ferry is carrying cars one may be asked to move from the W wall so that it can come in stern-to to unload.

The harbour is open to NE but if there is even a light wind anywhere between east and north there is an uncomfortable slop for small boats.

Facilities

A number of tavernas and cafés, and even a discotheque, are clustered around the waterfront. Most provisions are available.

A small boatyard, in the bay just to the NW of the light at the entrance, can haul out boats up to 1.5 m draught.

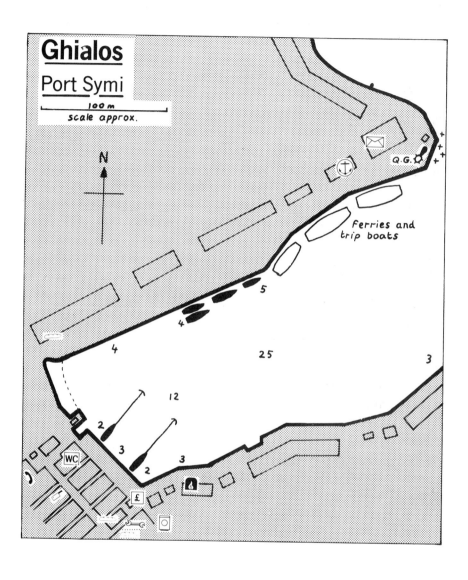

Ghialos

Port Symi

100 m
scale approx.

N

Q.G.

Ferries and
trip boats

5

4

25

3

4

12

2

3

3

2

WC

£

Port Symi, Ghialos

AGIOS EMILIANOS   36°36'.5N 27°46'.6E

A delightful little bay beside the monastery of Agios Emilianos, which sits on a tiny near-island connected to the Symi shore only by a short causeway.

On the opposite side of the bay, reached by a path, is the Monastery of Agios Filimanos.

There are no facilities here.

Mooring

Stern-to the little quay in front of the monastery, or anchored in the NW corner of the bay. The bottom is sand with some stones, and shelves away steeply beyond the eastern end of the little quay.

This is not a particularly well-sheltered anchorage, and is only advisable in settled weather, or in southerly or south-west to westerly winds.

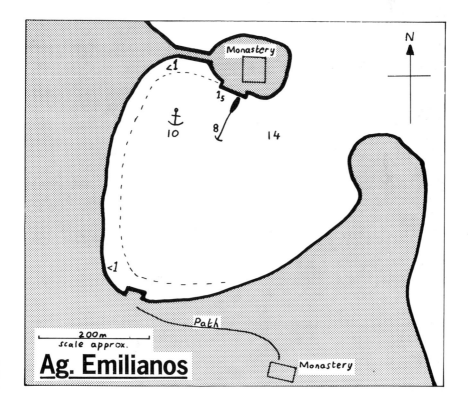

PANORMITIS   36°33′N 27°50′.7E

A peaceful and fairly well enclosed natural harbour, on the W coast of the island. The only habitation here is the Monastery of the Archangel

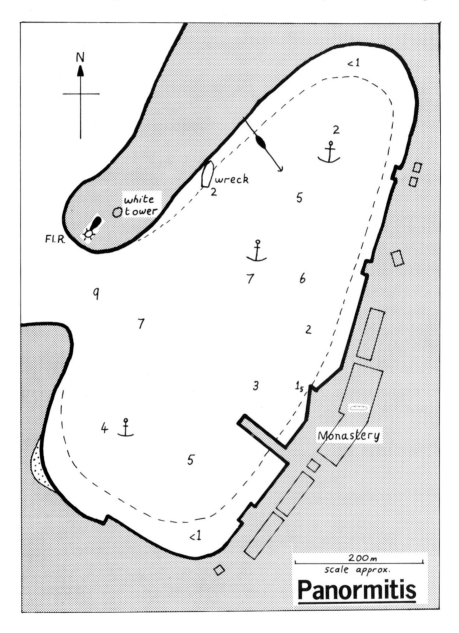

Panormitis

Michael of Panormitis with its blocks of hostel rooms, most of which lie empty in the winter months.

Approach and mooring

The entrance is marked by a light and a conspicuous short white tower with a red conical roof (an old windmill) on the N side of the mouth of the bay.

Anchor in the SW part of the bay off the little beach, or to the NE. Holding is good, on sand with patches of weed. Depths off the quay in front of the monastery are too shallow to lie stern-to, except possibly with a long stern line. The concrete pier is in constant daytime use by excursion boats.

In strong W or NW winds a rather uncomfortable swell can enter the bay, and strong variable gusts will sweep to and fro.

It is possible for a small yacht to lie securely alongside the wrecked fishing boat, where the depth is about 2 m.

Facilities

There are two simple tavernas, both of which sell some basic provisions, and also a baker.

MARATHONDA   36°34'.1N 27°51'.7E   (No plan)

An isolated inlet on the south-east shore of the island with a tiny community at its head, but with no facilities whatsoever.

As there is not sufficient room to swing, one should drop anchor in about 7 m, and take a stern line to the little concrete jetty.

The bay is open to the E and SE, and a strong NW'ly wind brings gusts down from the hills behind.

PEDI   36°37'N 27°51'.4E

A very attractive and unspoilt fishing village at the head of a narrow mile-long inlet just south from the main port, Ghialos.

There is a hotel under construction, but it seems halted indefinitely at the familiar Greek 'concrete frame' stage.

A twenty minute walk up the road brings you to the island's capital, Horio, on the hill, and a further fifteen minutes down to the main harbour on the other side.

The ferry to the islands calls here.

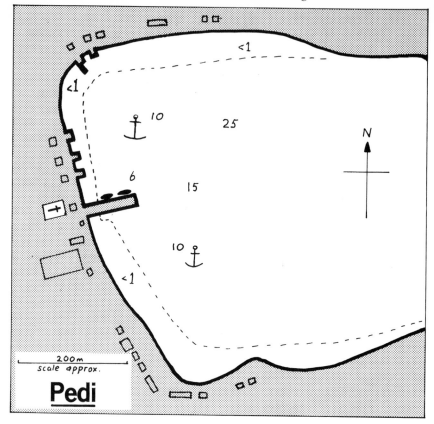

Pedi

Mooring
Unfortunately the bottom is rocky and deep so that anchoring securely is almost impossible. However, depths are quite sufficient to lie alongside the concrete jetty, but bear in mind day-trip boats also moor here, usually to the south side of it, and only during the day; and the ferry, when it arrives, goes stern-to the end. The inlet is open only to the east.

Facilities
There are two quite simple tavernas in the season, and limited provisions are available.

CHAPTER 24

Halki and Alimnia

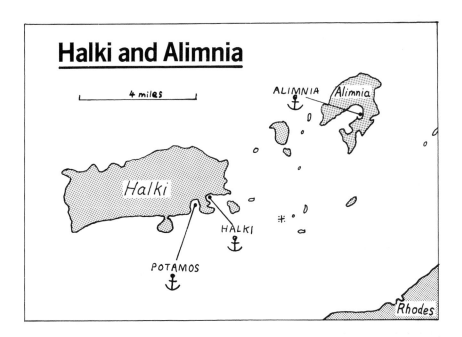

Harbours and anchorages

	Open to:	Comments:
Halki (harbour)	SE/E/NE	Poor in strong S'ly winds
Potamos	SE/S/SW	–
Alimnia	SW	Some swell in strong S'ly or W'ly winds

HALKI   36°13'.3N 27°36'.8E

Lying only three miles off the west coast of Rhodes, Halki provides a useful shelter from NW'ly winds, and is a good point from which to set off

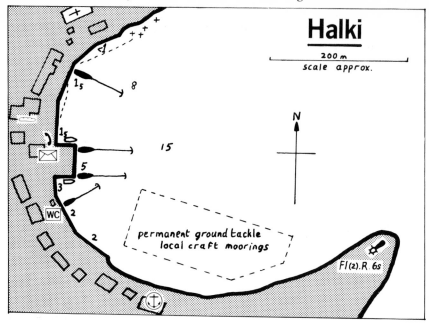

towards Karpathos or Crete. The only village on the island, with its reasonably well sheltered harbour, has a certain quiet unspoilt charm and is worth a visit.

The walk to the castle with its splendid view takes about two hours, and another one and a half hours on a mule track brings you to the monastery, with an apparently lone and almost self-sufficient monk, on the far side of the island.

Mooring

Stern-to at various points on the quay where depths permit. The bottom is stony and rather poor holding. Care should be taken towards the SW side not to get entangled with the ground tackle of the permanent moorings of local boats.

Boats that run to and from Kamirou Skala on Rhodes generally moor alongside the projecting quay. Once or twice a week a larger ferry comes in briefly, stern-to the end of this projection.

The harbour is open to the east, and in NE to SE winds it is best to move across to Alimnia. The surge in a S'ly or SW'ly can be uncomfortable, rebounding off the island at the mouth of the bay into the harbour.

Facilities

✚ ✉ ↘ ⌒

Most provisions can be bought, and there are about half a dozen cafes and tavernas in the season. Fresh water is very limited, but can be drawn from the well in the church courtyard.

POTAMOS   36°13′.2N 26°36′.1E

A pleasant summer anchorage just around the point from Halki, open to the south. There is one taverna on the shore, and a five minute walk brings you to Halki village.

When anchoring, keep well clear of the rock with 2 m depth over it in the centre of the bay. The bottom is sand and shingle.

The two large bollards set in the rock to NE are for the tanker which delivers fuel for the island's generator. The excessive tar on the beach, which should be cleared away in summer, apparently collects here due to this fuel delivery.

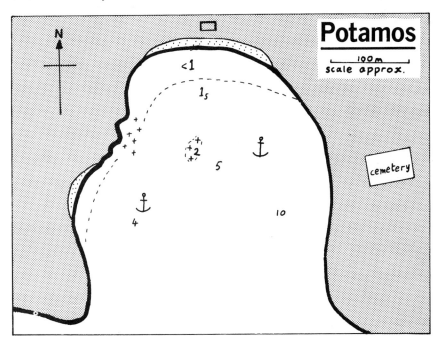

ALIMNIA   36°15′.8N 27°42′E

The large inlet to the SW of the island used to support a small community, but now seems practically deserted.

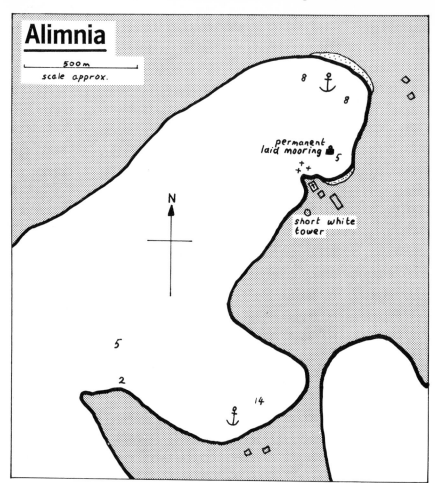

The anchorage at Alimnia

One can anchor here in very peaceful surroundings either in the extreme S part of the bay, although the bottom is rather steep-to, or to the NE. The best mooring here is close E of the little white chapel, but note that there is a concrete permanent mooring block with chain and line attached in this area, which was laid for a seaplane but is now almost never used.

In very strong NW winds some swell may reach the head of the inlet, and strong gusts come from all directions. The bottom is sand, with a little weed, with depths of 4–7 m.

CHAPTER 25

Rhodes

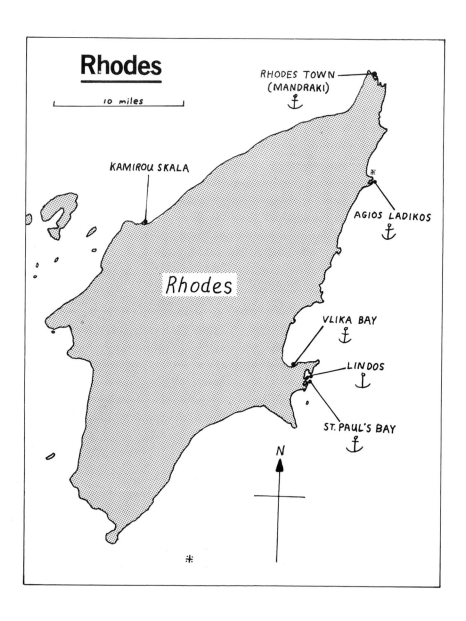

Rhodes

10 miles

RHODES TOWN
(MANDRAKI) ⚓

KAMIROU SKALA

AGIOS LADIKOS ⚓

Rhodes

VLIKA BAY ⚓

LINDOS ⚓

ST. PAUL'S BAY ⚓

N

Harbours and anchorages

	Open to:	Comments:
Mandraki (Rhodes Town harbour) Port of Entry	–	Entrance difficult in very strong SE winds
Kamirou Skala (quay)	N/NE/E	Also poor in strong NW winds
Lindos	E/SE	–
St. Paul's Bay	NE	Entrance difficult in E/SE winds
Vlika Bay	NE	–
Agios Ladikos	E/NE	Entrance difficult in strong S/SE winds

Anyone coming to Rhodes today expecting to find a beautiful, rich, exotic island, the 'daughter of Venus', is bound to be disappointed. Nowadays one has to look hard, and with heavily blinkered eyes, to see what remains of the beauty and culture of the Rhodes depicted in books and travelogues of years past.

Whilst cultivation on the island is in sad decline as the population moves into the more lucrative business of serving tourism, Rhodes town has been transformed, mushrooming into a sprawling holiday resort with hotels, restaurants, bars, discotheques, and an almost unbelievable number of shops dealing in every kind of tourist-tempting merchandise, from mass produced ceramics and souvenirs, to fashionable French *haute côuture*, and furs.

Nevertheless there are enough interesting places to visit to make a trip into the interior of the island worthwhile, even if not for the picture of charming rural life of days gone by. In the hills one can however still find a scattering of unspoilt villages, and also the quite beautiful Valley of the Butterflies, tranquil and uncrowded outside the main holiday season.

The coast of the island outside the main town offers disappointingly few safe and attractive anchorages for a yacht. The principal one is Lindos with its sandy beach, its picturesque village and fine castle. Sadly, it is overrun with tourists for an unusually long season from March until well into October.

Apart from at Lindos and Rhodes town, there are a few other good beaches, situated on the E coast, including the superb Tsambika, with nearly 2 miles of beautiful sand, best visited by road since it is a completely exposed anchorage.

The island's airport is served by regular international charter and domestic flights, which include services to Crete and Cyprus.

From the ferry port next to Mandraki harbour there are ferries to all of the Dodecanese and many other Aegean islands, as well as Athens, Cyprus and Israel.

MANDRAKI (Rhodes Town)   36°27′N 28°13′.6E   Port of Entry

A safe harbour, but over-crowded for most of the season from May until the end of September, requiring yachts to moor in two or three ranks around its perimeter.

Conveniently situated right alongside the very centre of town, it inevitably can be rather noisy if moored on the W wall with the road running by only metres away.

The town itself is a busy holiday centre, as already described, but in the old walled city tourist traders are confined to the main streets. The rambling backstreets and alleyways are a delight, and remain almost entirely unchanged.

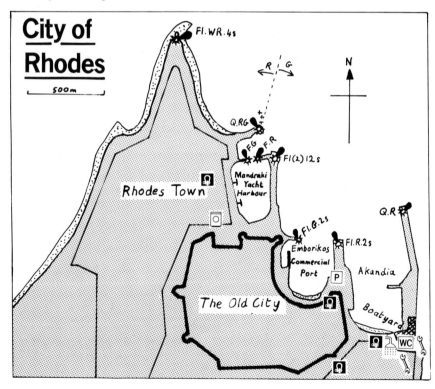

Approach and mooring

The three disused windmills and the fort just to the N of them are clearly identifiable when approached from NE to E, and the entrance is immediately to the right hand side of the fort. Coming from W or N keep a fair distance offshore until the fort is identified, and particularly keep clear of the submerged rocks off the short spit to the N of the fort. Entering between this spit and the fort, one turns immediately left between the two breakwaters into the harbour basin itself.

This approach is only difficult in strong SE winds when there is swell and even some surf running at the entrance. Nevertheless if one can ride this swell under reduced power and still maintain directional control until the hard turn to S to pass between the breakwaters, the entrance is by no means impossible.

For most of the year, space for yachts is grossly insufficient, and in addition there is a floating restaurant occupying valuable berthing space on the S wall, even though Rhodes has more than enough restaurants elsewhere.

It is often not possible to find a clear section of wall to go stern-to; one therefore has to lay the anchor and then drop back, securing the stern to the bows of boats already moored. It is accepted that you will have to pass to and fro across their decks to get ashore.

In this way many yachts can hardly be said to have a proper berth, and thankfully mooring charges are correspondingly low. Charter operators seem to pay for reserved spaces on the wall, most of these being towards the S end of the east breakwater. It is best not to moor here as one is bound to be asked to move as charterers arrive and depart.

Situated on the tip of the island, the wind always blows stronger here in the harbour than further out to sea. Nevertheless it is safe enough in any wind for yachts to stay here afloat in the winter if attended, the worst conditions being the SE'ly gales, when waves break over the E breakwater, and the swell running at the entrance creates quite a surge inside the harbour.

Facilities

plus officials for a Port of Entry.

Arriving either in transit or from abroad, ships papers should be presented at the customs office in the SE corner of Mandraki. The transit log will then be delivered to the Port Captain's office in the opposite corner of the harbour, and it is from there that it should be collected when departing. The passport office is unfortunately situated some distance

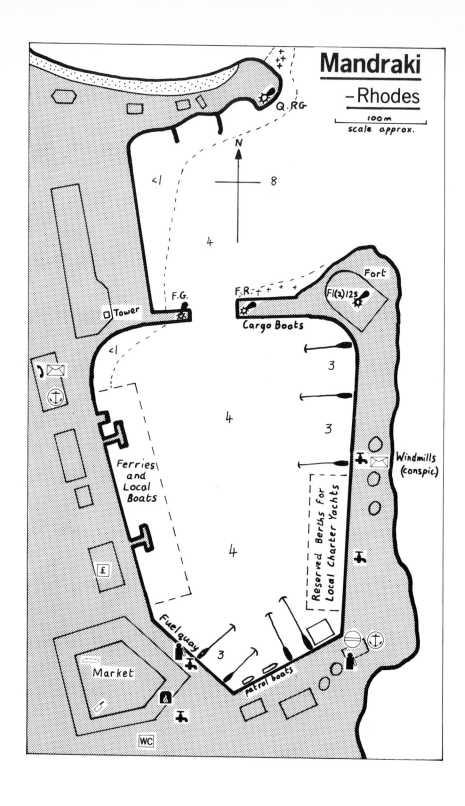

Mandraki
–Rhodes

100m
scale approx.

Q.RG

N

< 1

8

4

F.G.

F.R. + +

Fort

Fl(2)12s

£3

Cargo Boats

< 1

3

Tower

4

3

Ferries
and
Local
Boats

Windmills
(conspic.)

4

Reserved Berths for
Local Charter Yachts

£

4

Fuel quay

3

Market

patrol boats

WC

away in the commercial port. Including the walk, one needs to allow about an hour to complete clearance formalities for leaving the country. The offices usually open around 08.30. It is possible to obtain clearance the previous evening if leaving early in the morning.

There are a few water points around the harbour, often requiring a long hose to reach the boat, and the attendant who has the key can be hard to find. If so, enquire at the port office. Electricity is also provided at several points on the E wall.

Fuel can be taken aboard directly from the fuel quay in the SW corner. Ask at the fuel office beside the customs post. In summer when space in the harbour is very limited, larger yachts are often allowed to remain moored at the fuel quay longer than merely for refuelling purposes. This can cause difficulties for other yachts requiring fuel. As an alternative, fuel can be delivered by bowser, or collected by canister from the service station only 100 m from the fuel quay.

The depot for bottled gas is some way away, but one or two of the shops around the market will take bottles and arrange for them to be refilled.

Shops for all provisions are conveniently close. Chandlers (apart from the Camper and Nicholson agency a short way up from the market) are between the commercial port and the boatyard. For sail repairs, enquire at the charter operators.

At the boatyard there is ample hard standing, and hauling out facilities include a Travel Hoist with a weight limit of 50 tons, but continual silting of the area often restricts draught to as little as 2 m and has been known to cause re-launching problems.

There is a British Consul in the town, and also consulates of a few other countries, including Turkey.

Because Rhodes enjoys a special duty status, liquor is as cheap here as one can find anywhere. For this reason, when arriving from abroad there is no point in bringing duty free liquor with you.

One other amenity worth a visit is the Turkish style bath house or *humub*, in the old city, especially welcome after a particularly cold wet beginning- or end-of-season passage.

KAMIROU SKALA   36°16'.5N 27°49'.5E   (No plan)

This is the only place providing any sort of shelter on the W coast of the island, but even here protection is very poor, and it is not recommended to stay overnight. As a place to get ashore however, it can be useful.

The quay is on the E side of a short promontory, and lies five miles east of Alimnia island. A yacht can moor alongside in 3–4 m. There are a couple of small tavernas nearby.

Boats run to and fro from here to Halki, some 10 miles distant.

The quay is open up the coast to the NE, and there is almost always some swell alongside in any wind direction.

LINDOS   36°05′.8N 28°05′.3E

The very fine restored castle of the knights of St. John, and the pretty village of Lindos, are two of the principal tourist attractions on Rhodes. Unfortunately, the sheer number of visitors, and the noise in the evening from the tavernas on the beach, inevitably detract from what would otherwise be a charming and highly attractive place. The situation in the village is slightly improved in the evening when the daytime visitors have mostly returned to Rhodes Town. But still it is clearly a village given to the holiday trade, and there is little if any real Greek village life remaining.

Approach and mooring

The fortress standing high on a promontory is clearly visible from 3 or 4 miles off, and the mouth of Lindos Bay, partially closed off on its N side by two rocky islets, lies just N of it. Entrance is possible to the N of the two islets, but the area of deep water is rather narrow and it is better to enter to the S of them.

Anchor either in the SW arm of the bay close to the village, off the sandy beach with several tavernas on the shore, or in the quieter but rocky NW arm. In the SW part there are one or two water-skiing areas to keep clear of in the season; these are not easily identified as they are not marked or buoyed off.

Shelter is good, but the bay is open to the E, and in strong SE winds in early and late season it is not advisable to stay here. Some further protection can be gained by small yachts behind the stone breakwater extending NW on the SE side of the bay, but depths are only sufficient towards its outer end, and there is only space for one or two boats. The buoy off the end of this breakwater marks a permanent laid mooring used by excursion boats from Rhodes during the day, to moor and land passengers on the breakwater.

Facilities

£ ✚ ✉ ↘ ⌐ ▣

Several tavernas on the beach and in the village, where there are also

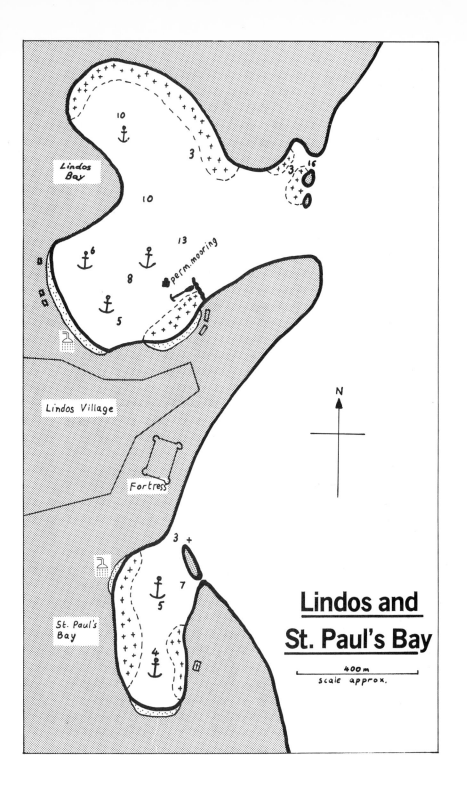

Lindos
Bay

10 ⚓

3

3 16

10

13
6 ⚓
⚓
perm.mooring
8
⚓
5

Lindos Village

Fortress

N

St. Paul's
Bay

3 +

7
⚓
5

4
⚓

Lindos and
St. Paul's Bay

400 m
scale approx.

shops for most provisions. Motorbikes and cars can be hired, and buses run regularly to Rhodes Town.

There are cold showers on the main beach.

ST. PAUL'S BAY – Lindos   36°05′.2N 28°05′.3E

Immediately south beneath the castle is the narrow rocky entrance to this charming and almost landlocked bay, with a small sandy beach at its southern end. This is a much quieter anchorage than the main Lindos bay, but in the high season yachts have often been asked to leave for fear of pollution, since it is very enclosed.

Depths are adequate over most of the bay, but care should be taken to stay clear of the underwater rocks in several areas around the perimeter, particularly on the W side. There is room for a small yacht to swing, but a stern line could be taken to a rock ashore at various points. The bottom is sand, with some stony patches and a few rocks to be avoided.

Protection is almost all-round. Only very strong E or SE winds would throw a heavy swell at the entrance, and I have not personally experienced conditions inside the bay in such weather to know if the surge could be dangerous. The entrance would certainly be impossible.

St. Paul's Bay, Lindos

VLIKA BAY   36°06′.3N 28°04′.3E   (No plan)

This bay, 1½ miles to the west of the point just north of Lindos Bay, provides a reasonable shelter, much better than Lindos, in strong S or SE winds. Towards the SE end of the beach is a large white hotel, and right in the SE corner, a concrete aquaduct. For best protection tuck into this corner as closely as possible, but proceed with care as the bottom is very gently shelving with only 4 m depth some 400 m offshore. Anchor in 4–7 m on sand.

This anchorage is wide open from N to E and is only recommended as a protection from S to SE winds, and not in any other conditions.

AGIOS LADIKOS   36°19′.6N 28°12′.8E   (No plan)

Lying approximately 9 miles down the E coast of the island from Rhodes Town, this quite well sheltered bay provides an interesting and secluded anchorage, but should be treated with some caution due to the uneven and rocky bottom.

The entrance is right at the tip of Agios Ladikos point, and the inlet extends to the SW. There is a broken concrete pier on the left just inside the mouth, and beyond it, towards the S side of the bay and at the head, are boulders and submerged rocks, so one should not proceed very far past the pier.

There are anchoring depths of 5–12 m on a bottom of mainly sand, but with some stones and rocks, so the anchor may not set first time. There is space for a small yacht to swing, but a stern line can be run out in several places, either to a rock or to the broken pier. Open from E to N, but quite well protected from other directions.

Caution: An isolated rocky shoal with only 4 m depth over it lies about 1 mile from the mouth of Agios Ladikos bay in an approximately NNE'ly direction. This could be dangerous to most yachts in a heavy swell.

Part Four

THE TURKISH COAST
– MARMARIS TO ANTALYA

CHAPTER 26

Marmaris to Gulf of Fethiye

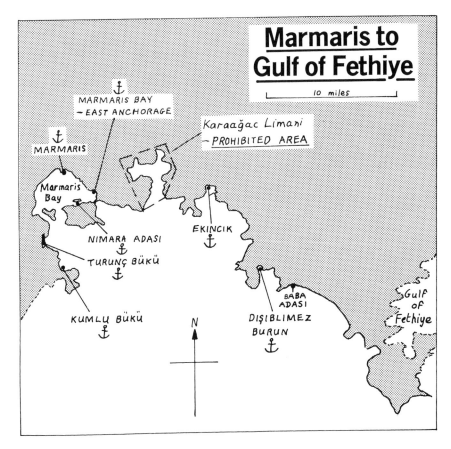

Harbours and anchorages

	Open to:	Comments:
Marmaris (quay)	S/SE	Further protection behind a tiny mole for only 3–4 yachts
Marmaris Bay, E anchorage	SE	Only for a short fetch of less than 1 mile
Marmaris Bay, Nimara Adasi	NW	–

	Open to:	Comments:
Turunç Bükü	NE/E/SE	–
Kumlu Bükü	N/NE/E	Also deflected swell in S'ly winds
Ekincik	S/SE	Fair protection from SE is possible across the bay
Dişiblimez Burun	SW/S/SE	–
Baba Adasi	W/E	Rebound swell in strong S'ly winds

MARMARIS   28°16'.5N 36°51'.1E   Port of Entry

Despite having no proper yacht harbour, Marmaris is something of a focal point for the yachting scene in this area. This is largely thanks to its position close to the popular gulfs of Doris and Kos to the N, and of Fethiye to the E, but also because it is the closest Turkish Port of Entry to Rhodes, only 25 miles away to the S.

Marmaris town is on the N side of a large, wooded and almost land-locked bay, some 3 miles wide, with a number of quite big hotels lining the W shore, catering for the increasing numbers of mainly Turkish holidaymakers that visit here in the summer season.

Nevertheless, despite the growing tourist trade Marmaris manages to retain a very typically Turkish flavour, and together with the group of anchorages in and around the bay is a very pleasant place to spend a few days.

Approach and mooring

Entering the bay, Marmaris town with its conspicuous minarets and small castle comes into view on the opposite shore. The quays for visiting yachts are at the right hand end of the town, either on the stretch of quay immediately W of the tip of the short promontory, or around to the E side of it. In summer, the predominant wind blows across the bay from the west, or even slightly south of west, and tends to be stronger in the bay and approaches than further out to sea. This can set up quite a chop, which makes the sections of the quay both on the W side of the promontory and between its S tip and the tiny harbour just on its E side, quite uncomfortable, except for large yachts. In such conditions the stretch of quay further up the E side, beyond the minute harbour, is preferable; but one has to approach with care as the depths decrease sharply 2–3 m from the quay wall, which is itself in a rather poor state of repair in parts. It is possible to go stern-to at one or two points, but because of the unevenness close to the wall it is advisable to go bows-to if possible to avoid risk of damaging the rudder.

The small harbour to the W of the promontory and the stretch of quay to the W of that are reserved for local boats.

There is space for 4 or 5 yachts inside the little harbour on the E side of the promontory, which is also the only place to gain protection from the fierce SE'ly winds that blow at the beginning and end of the season. A few yachts do in fact winter here.

If there is no suitable space on the quay, there are convenient depths to

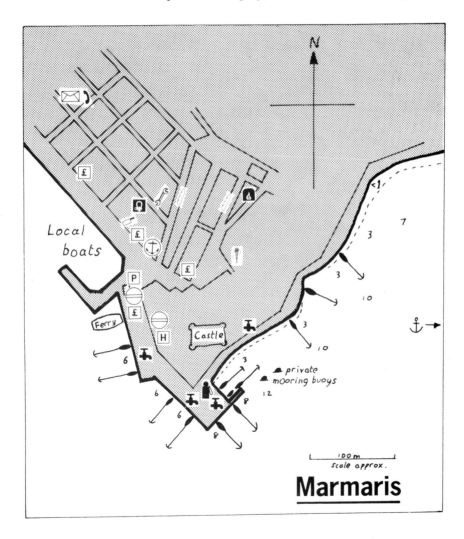

Local boats

Ferry

Castle

private
mooring buoys

100 m
scale approx.

Marmaris

anchor over most of the area on the E side of the promontory between the town and the boatyards, where shelter is also fairly good from the predominant W'ly summer wind. In strong S winds, one should move to one of the other anchorages described below around Marmaris Bay.

Facilities

🚶 ⚓ ⛟ ❄ £ 🛢 ⚒ ⚓ ✚ D ✉ ➘ ⌒ ✎ ◤

plus officials for a Port of Entry

Water and electricity points are provided on the stretches of quay to both sides of the S tip of the promontory. To use them, ask at the harbour-master's office. Diesel is also on the quay by the tiny E harbour, but only in the season. At other times it must be collected by canister from the service station at the back of the town. Turkish and Camping gas bottles can be exchanged.

In and around town are numerous restaurants, bars, cafes, and good shops for provisions. There is also a sail repairer, and although the chandlers have only limited stocks of equipment, there is a machine shop capable of fabricating most stainless steel fittings to order at reasonable cost. Market day is Saturday.

Facilities for hauling out small and medium sized yachts are close to the town, and also on the opposite side of the bay behind Bedir Adasi.

MARMARIS BAY – East anchorage   36°49'.7N 28°18'.8E   (No plan)

On the far E side of Marmaris Bay there are two anchorages, together they offer protection from winds of any direction. To the N, tucked in behind a small promontory, anchor just left of a white hotel in 6–10 m on mud and weed, and if wished, run out a stern line to a pine tree on shore to the NW. Protection here from W and N winds is excellent, but in a very strong S wind one may prefer the opposite shore to the SSW where again one can anchor and swing, or run out a stern line to a tree on the SE shore.

MARMARIS BAY – Nimara Adasi   36°48'.9N 28°17'E   (No plan)

On the opposite side of the bay from Marmaris town is a well sheltered anchorage in a cove on Nimara Adasi, behind the small islet Bedir Adasi.

There are a few buildings and one or two restaurants on the shore. Anchor close to the beach taking care to keep clear of a few rocks close in. Depths are 8–18 m on a quite steep-shelving bottom of sand and weed, with room to swing.

Protection from the S is excellent, and close in to the shore one can also gain fairly good shelter from the W.

In 1984 a small boatyard was being set up here.

TURUNÇ BÜKÜ   24°46'.6N 28°15'.1E   (No plan)

Just outside the entrance to Marmaris Bay, on the W shore, is this attractive anchorage lying at the foot of steep hills that rise up behind a small village with a few restaurants on the beach. The best position is at the southern end of the beach, where additional shelter from the SE is provided by a short spur extending N. One is then fairly well protected from most directions, the most likely disturbance being the rebounding swell in the event of S or SE winds.

Although the guests in a W'ly wind off the hills to the W are notorious in this area, they appear to be at their worst between $\frac{1}{2}$ mile and 2 miles of the coast; they are not usually troublesome close in to the beach and in the anchorage.

The bottom is gently shelving, and anchoring depths are 3–6 m on sand and weed. Take care to avoid the rock less than a metre beneath the surface close in under the cliff in the SW corner. There are some mooring buoys in this area provided by the restaurants nearby, which can be picked up.

KUMLU BÜKÜ   36°45'N 28°16'.3E   (No plan)

Although not as well protected as Turunç Bükü (2 miles to the NNW), there being often some swell from SE, or from Marmaris Bay in strong NW winds, this is a reasonable place to spend the night by virtue of the moorings provided during the season by the Yat Kulubu restaurant in the SW corner of the bay. The wind here, close in under the steep hills, is very variable, but not normally unduly gusty or severe. The buoys should not be taken on deck as they have only a short scope of cable connecting them to the ground blocks. Pass a line through the loop in the strop and take it back on board. It is then recommended to take a stern line ashore to one of the mooring stakes provided on the beach. The moorings are safe for yachts up to about 32 ft. Alternatively one can anchor, the bottom being

coarse sand with weed patches and gently shelving, with depths of 4–7 m.
  Showers are provided at the restaurant.

**Caution: There is an isolated submerged rock with less than 2 m
depth over it on the W edge of the prohibited anchoring area
described below. It is named Turnalikayasi on Turkish charts, and
lies 1 mile off the mainland shore, just over 1½ miles W of the islet
Yilancik Adasi.**

Note: Karaağaç Limani, the very large bay 8 miles E of Marmaris, is
prohibited to yachts. It is also prohibited to anchor in the area around the
mouth of the bay, including the island Yilancik Adasi, although passage
through this area is allowed.

**Caution: Approaching Ekincik from W, there are several rocks,
mostly visible above water, as you come around Kizil Burun point
turning into Ekincik bay. But ⅔ mile N from the tip of this point
there is a dangerous rock only 1 m beneath the surface, approximately 100 m offshore.**

EKINCIK   36°49′.8N 28°33′.2E   (No plan)

An attractive and popular anchorage, in pine wooded surroundings, off a
sandy beach with a restaurant in summer. Anchor off the beach on a

Rock tombs, Dalyan River

gently shelving bottom of sand, with weed further off, in depths of 3–8 m with ample room for a number of yachts to swing. Well protected from N and W, but open to S and SE.

Some protection can be gained from S in the cove close by to the SE enclosed by a short spur on its S side, but the sea-bed is rather steep-to. Anchor here in 10–20 m with a stern line to a rock or tree to the SE. If W or N winds are only light to moderate, this anchorage is still satisfactory, but if they become stronger it is better to move to the NW and anchor off the main beach.

One of the main attractions of Ekincik is the river trips in summer operated by a fleet of small motor boats to the Dalyan river. One trip, lasting all day, includes stops at the ruins of ancient Caunus, and the hot sulphur springs, and passes by some impressive ancient rock tombs carved into the sheer cliff face. If you hail one of the boats as they pass by in the morning they will pick you up from your yacht. The trip makes a very relaxing day's outing, with a lunch stop at one of the picturesque riverside restaurants amongst the reeds, or you can take your own picnic.

DIŞIBLIMEZ BURUN   36°43′.2N 28°38′.9E   (No plan)

A striking and isolated anchorage in a steep-sided cove with partly rocky shores contrasting with pine wooded slopes. It lies approximately $1\frac{1}{2}$ miles NNE of the tip of cape Disiblimez Burun.

In the NE corner of the cove, a large rock standing above the surface obstructs the area off the small beach and makes anchoring unsuitable. To the NW is another beach, of grey sand, and one can anchor off this in 6–15 m on sand with some stones and small rocks. Close to the shore to the north, between the two beaches, are underwater rocks to be avoided.

The cove is open to the south. Being heavily enclosed on three sides, in prevailing W or N winds the anchorage often gets variable gusts, but these are not usually strong.

BABA ADASI   36°41′.7N 28°41′.8E   (No plan)

Here, 10 miles NW of the W side of the mouth of the Gulf of Fethiye is reasonable shelter from S, behind the islet Baba Adasi.

Entering the anchorage from W or E, keep close to the islet and well away from the sandy beach on the mainland shore as the sand shelf extends some way out, with only 2 m depths some 100 m off the beach. Approaching from W keep clear of underwater rocks close to the NW of the islet, and note that the maximum depth here between the islet and the sand shelf is only 4 m.

The approach from E is clear of obstructions, and the depth is around 10 m.

Anchor tight in behind the islet in 8–10 m on sand, with a stern line to the islet.

There is no real protection from the predominant W'ly summer winds, but as a shelter from S the anchorage can be useful and is fairly good.

CHAPTER 27

Gulf of Fethiye (Fethiye Körfezi)

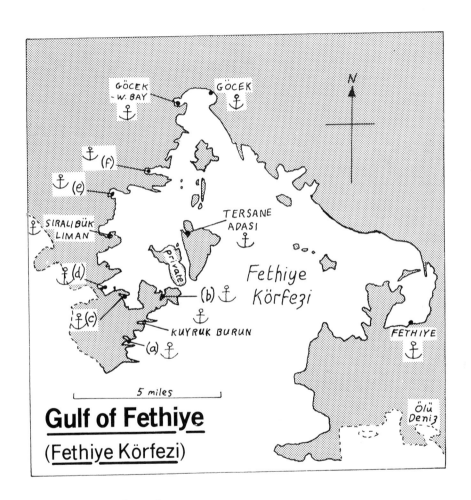

Gulf of Fethiye

(Fethiye Körfezi)

Harbours and anchorages

	Open to:	Comments:
Anchorage (a)	E/SE	Some swell in S winds
Kuyruk Burun	SE/E	Rebound swell in S winds
Tersane Adasi	NW	–

	Open to:	Comments:
Anchorage (b) ('4-fathom bay')	NW	–
Anchorage (c)	SE	For fetch of less than 1 mile. Rebound swell in strong N winds
Anchorage (d)	E	–
Siralibük Liman	–	Some swell in strong NE winds
Anchorage (e)	E/SE	–
Anchorage (f)	E	Some swell in strong SE or NE winds
Göcek	S/SW	Swell in strong SE winds
Göcek, west bay	–	–
Fethiye (quay)	N/NE	Better protection from N in anchorage close by

ANCHORAGE (a)   36°37'.2N 28°52'.1E   (No plan)

The most southerly of the anchorages on the W side of the gulf, this isolated inlet lies one mile north of Kazilkuyruk Burun point. It divides into two arms; one to the NW, but the better anchorage is in the arm to the W in 10–15 m depths on weed and sand, with a stern line to a rock as there is insufficient room to swing.

The NW arm is narrower, and more gently shelving with only 10 m depths 100 m from the beach at the head. The bottom is weed and sand, but with some patches of stones and small rocks. A stern line is essential.

Both arms are exposed to swell from E and SE.

KUYRUK BURUN   36°37'.9N 28°52'.9E   (No plan)

Anchorage in a deep bay on the S side of Kuyruk Burun point. Pine and olive trees cover the slopes around the inlet, and there is a small beach at the head. Anchor in 15–20 m, on sand and weed with some small rocks here and there. Run out a stern line, as there is just too little room to swing.

Open to SE and E.

TERSANE ADASI   36°40'.6N 28°54'.9E

Personally, my favourite anchorage in the gulf, in a small well sheltered inlet at the NW point of Tersane Adasi island. The bay is uninhabited, and has some attractive and interesting ruins with a few palm trees on the shore. There are also remains of the walls of a tiny harbour in the E corner, and one should not approach this area too closely as there are rocks here and there beneath the surface.

Anchor as shown on the plan, either with a stern line to the S shore, or around towards the harbour remains, where shelter is better, with a stern line to a tree to the N. The bottom is sand and weed.

Protection in most conditions is very good, the narrow entrance being open only to the NW.

Note: Domuz Adasi island just to the west of Tersane Adasi island is private, and landing is prohibited.

Both the channel between Domuz Adasi and Tersane Adasi and the tiny channel at the southern tip of Domuz Adasi have ample depth for safe passage.

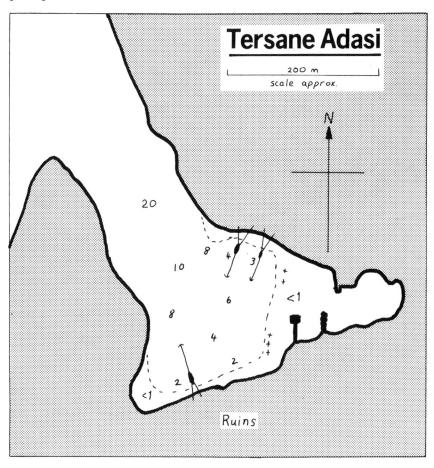

ANCHORAGE (b) ('4-fathom bay')   36°38′.7N 28°53′.6E

A small narrow inlet, close S of Domuz Adasi island, uninhabited except for one tiny restaurant which operates in the season.

A concreted quay on the E shore is not very suitable for mooring, being shallow close to, and having no rings for mooring lines.

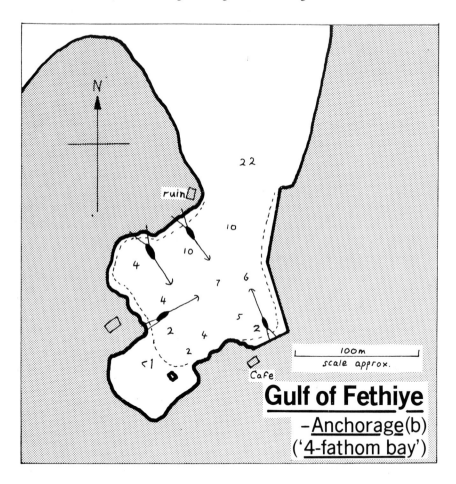

Gulf of Fethiye
–Anchorage(b)
('4-fathom bay')

Anchor around to the right just inside the entrance, and take a stern line ashore to the W. The bottom is sand. Take care to stay clear of the shallow area in the SW corner.

Protection from most directions is good, except for a swell that can enter in strong northerly winds.

ANCHORAGE (c) 36°38′.5N 28°51′.9E (No plan)

A very pretty anchorage in a tiny cove tucked around the NW corner of the bay 1 mile W of '4-fathom bay'. There is space for 4 or 5 yachts to anchor with stern lines to the stone quay in front of a tiny summer restaurant almost hidden in the trees. Anchoring depths are 12–20 m, and the bottom is sand and light weed. Open only to SE for a short fetch of less than 1 mile.

ANCHORAGE (d) 36°38′.7N 28°51′.1E (No plan)

A quite large bay, 2 miles SW of Domuz Adasi, with an attractive and secluded anchorage to W or S at the head. In the far west corner a small restaurant operates in summer, in a charming setting, almost hidden in the olive groves.

Tuck right into the corner, just past the restaurant, and anchor in 10–18 m on soft sand with light weed, with a stern line to a tree. Alternatively, in the extreme S corner of the bay, anchor off the ruin at the water's edge with a stern line to a tree, but note that the sea-bed here is very steep-to, and one has to let go the anchor in 20 m or more.

Both anchorages are open to the NE.

SIRALIBÜK LIMAN 36°40′.5N 28°51′.8E (No plan)

The bay Siralibük Liman lies 2½ miles W of the anchorage at the N of Tersane Adasi. Immediately as you enter the mouth of the bay, there is a small cove tucked around to the left hand side, out of sight until you are abreast of it, providing a very well sheltered and secluded anchorage.

The bottom shelves steeply until quite close in, then becomes very shallow 30 m from the beach. Lay out the anchor close to the shore to the NE in 12–20 m, and haul in the stern with a line to a tree on the opposite shore to the SW. The sea-bed is soft sand with some weed.

Protection is practically all-round except for a swell that works into the anchorage in strong NE winds.

ANCHORAGE (e) 36°41′.8N 28°51′.9E (No plan)

Here, in the bay 1 mile to the N of Siralibük Liman, a short promontory with olive trees on its ridge extends out from the S shore protecting a pleasant anchorage in the SW corner of the bay. The bottom is steep-to until quite close in to the small beach just past the promontory. Anchor here in 6–18 m on weed and sand, and haul in the stern with a line to the shore to S.

A tiny café set in the trees on the beach serves simple meals in summer.

ANCHORAGE (f)   36°42'.6N 28°53'.7E   (No plan)

A longish inlet, W of the Yassica Adalari islets with a reasonably well sheltered anchorage in the SW corner at its head, to the left of a small summer restaurant nestling amongst the reeds. Stay clear of the reedy area right in the SW corner as the bottom shallows up very suddenly here.

Anchor in 12–20 m on mud, and haul in the stern with a line to a tree on the S shore. Shelter is reasonably good but swell from NE or S winds can work into the anchorage.

GÖCEK   36°45'.1N 28°56'.3E   (No plan)

This small town at the far N of the gulf is useful for provisioning, but otherwise is not of any special interest. There are shops for most food supplies, including a baker, and there is also a shop for Turkish bottled gas.

The large anchoring area off the village with depths of 3–6 m on mud, is very gently shelving so one should not approach too close to shore. For 2 or 3 yachts, drawing less than 2 m, there may be space to go bows-to the short concrete jetty in the centre of the village.

In summer this anchorage is normally quite satisfactory, but it is open to S, and in the event of S'ly winds one should move to the anchorage in the W bay (*below*).

GÖCEK, West Bay   36°45'.28N 28°55'.7E   (No plan)

A very safe and quite pleasant anchorage (despite a commercial wharf with storage tanks and a warehouse on the N shore) lying just W of Göcek village, immediately on the W side of the point on which stands the Göcek Inner Harbour light.

Anchor only in the E half of the bay as the W part is silted and very shallow. A wreck lies at the limit of the shallow area. There is also a wreck in the extreme S corner of the bay.

Depths are 8–15 m on a bottom of mud, with room to swing and all round protection.

FETHIYE   36°37′.4N 29°06′E   Port of Entry

A fair sized town, with a slowly growing tourism trade, providing useful facilities and communications links for cruising yachts.

Approach and mooring

To enter the bay Fethiye Limani, the main channel is to the S of the island Fethiye Adasi, but the narrow channel to the NW is also navigable although there are some marked wrecks to be avoided. Once inside the bay the town will be seen on the shore to the S, and the yacht quay is at the W end of the built up area.

The E side of the bay is heavily silted for some way out from the low lying shore, in some places as much as half way across the full width. The limit of the shallowest area, in the SE corner, is marked by two buoys, but in any case it is best to keep well over towards the W shore when crossing the bay.

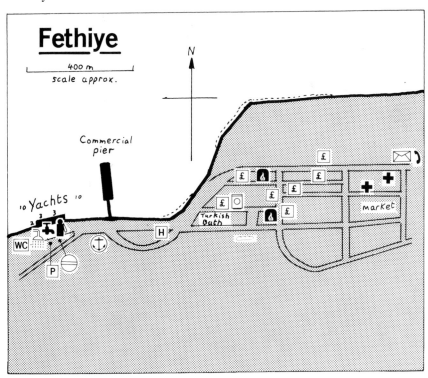

Moor stern-to the yacht quay, which is just to the W of the commercial pier. Protection is usually fairly good, except in a N or NE blow, when quite a chop can be set up in the two mile length of the bay, causing some disturbance at the quay. In such conditions it is safer to move to the anchorage immediately to the NW, where depths are 5–6 m, and the bottom is mud and weed.

Facilities

plus officials for a Port of Entry

There are fuel pumps on the quay but, if these are not in use, fuel can be obtained by the dock master who will arrange for canisters to be filled at the service station. At the gas shop, gas is only exchangeable in Turkish bottles, but other bottles can be filled.

Market day (with a fascinating bazaar), is on Mondays.

From the bus station there are services to most major towns as well as all of the surrounding area. Dalaman airport is nearby, with the majority of commercial passenger flights being holiday charters from Europe. There are however also domestic flights fairly regularly to the few other Turkish big city airports.

CHAPTER 28

Fethiye to Kaş

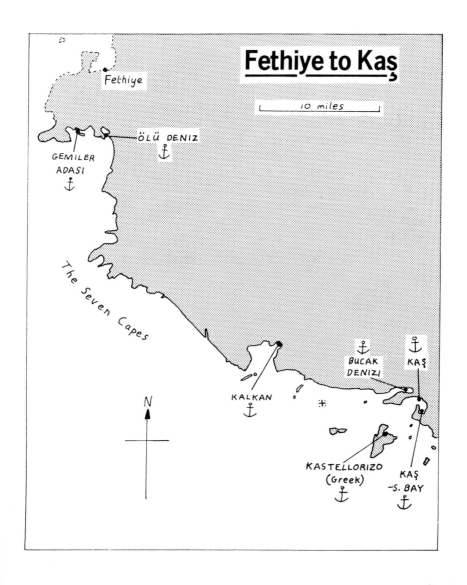

Fethiye to Kaş

10 miles

Fethiye

ÖLÜ DENIZ

GEMILER
ADASI

The Seven Capes

N

KALKAN

BUCAK
DENIZI

KAŞ

KASTELLORIZO
(Greek)

KAŞ
-S. BAY

Harbours and anchorages

	Open to:	Comments:
Gemiler Adasi	–	Swell in strong S winds
Ölü Deniz	SE	Emergency protection from south inside lagoon
Kalkan (harbour)	–	Entrance difficult in very strong S'ly winds
Bucak Denizi	W	–
Kastellorizo (harbour) **Greek**	N/NE	–
Kaş	S/SW	Swell in strong W winds
Kaş, south bay	N	For short fetch across to Kaş

GEMILER ADASI   36°33'.4N 29°03'.8E   (No plan)

A very pleasant anchorage offering good shelter, 2½ miles W of Ölü Deniz. It is possible to moor in the channel between Gemiler Adasi island and the mainland shore, but the depths are rather great for small to medium sized yachts. It is necessary to let go the anchor in 25 m or more, and probably advisable to swing, although a stern line could be run out to the island shore. With sufficient scope on the anchor cable this anchorage is quite safe, the only swell likely to enter being reflected in from strong S winds.

There are more reasonable anchoring depths and a charming anchorage in the little cove on the mainland shore opposite the W tip of the island. A pretty, very small restaurant operates in summer, situated in the olive grove on the beach.

Anchor in 7–15 m on sand, with room to swing, or tuck in to the left hand side, with a stern line to a rock or tree.

Partially open to S, this cove is not suitable in strong S winds.

ÖLÜ DENIZ   36°33'N 29°06'.8E

This is the famous lagoon depicted on tourist pamphlets, travel guide books, postcards, and posters on travel agents' walls all over Turkey. Although from certain positions the place does make a good photograph, you should not set your expectations too high if visiting in a yacht. The bank protecting the lagoon, which appears from a distance to be sand, turns out be gravel; the number of people on the beach during the day in summer compares with popular beaches in Spain, and at night the

Ölü Deniz

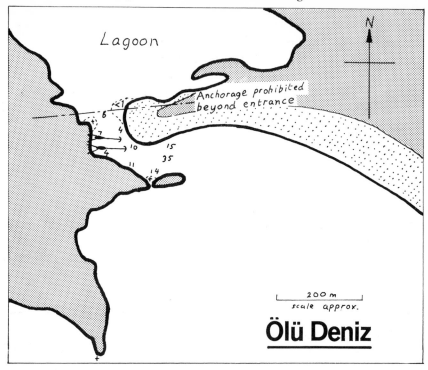

tranquillity is somewhat upset by loud music from the nearby hotel. As well as this, in the season at least, yachts are not permitted to anchor inside the lagoon, but are confined to the reasonable but limited shelter right at the entrance. Southerly swell causes some disturbance.

Moor as shown on the plan, anchoring on a sandy bottom with a stern line to a tree to the W. It is best to arrive in the evening, as during the daytime, in season, it is a little like trying to manoeuvre in the deep end of a busy municipal swimming pool.

There is no restaurant near the anchorage, but there is one around on the NE side of the lagoon.

In summer there are regular buses to Fethiye.

KALKAN   36°15'.8N 29°25'E

A charming small village, comprising a peculiar mixture of unsafe derelict houses damaged in an earthquake in 1968, and restored buildings many of which have been tastefully converted into delightful café-bars, restaurants and boarding houses.

Mooring

The harbour of rough rock breakwaters gives practically all round protection, with the only swell likely to occur in strong S'ly winds.

Some rocky areas around the perimeter of the harbour considerably restrict the areas suitable for mooring, there being only a few areas where it is possible for smaller yachts to moor close enough in, bows-to, to step ashore. Mooring points are very poor, and one has to make do with rocks or posts to secure lines in most cases.

In a heavy S'ly swell, the entrance can be difficult.

Facilities

A water pipe has been led to the NE side of the harbour just above the small concrete quay. Turkish gas bottles can be exchanged.

There are several good restaurants and cafés, and also shops for most provisions.

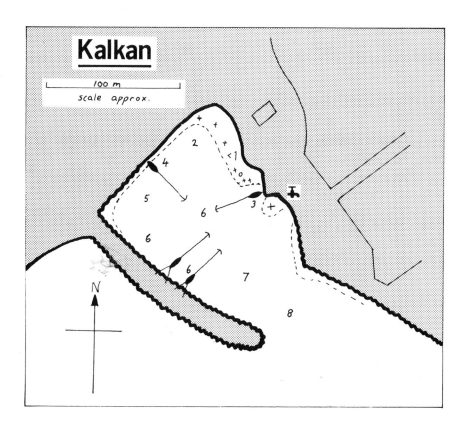

Caution: The isolated rock lying 1 mile off the coast, and 7¾ miles west of Kaş, is approximately 2 m beneath the surface.

BUCAK DENIZI   36°12′.2N 29°38′E   (No plan)

This 2½ mile long inlet, protected by a peninsula immediately to the west of Kaş, provides an unattractive but almost completely sheltered anchorage at its head, preferable to Kaş harbour in bad weather. Only in strong W winds is there some chop set up in the bay.

Anchor in 7 m plus on mud, at the head of the inlet, or in 12–20 m off the south shore ½ mile before the head.

Kaş village is a short walk just over the ridge.

KASTELLORIZO   36°04′.1N 29° 35′.5E   **Greek**

Kastellorizo is not a Port of Entry, and in theory therefore can only be visited by sailing down from Rhodes direct, some 70 miles away. In

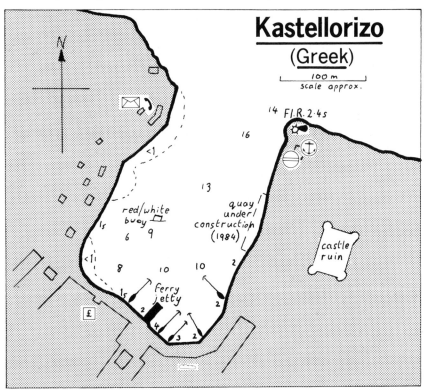

practice however there seems no objection to a yacht cruising in Turkey making a day trip to the island (changing courtesy flags before entering harbour) but it is not advisable to stay overnight. Small motor boats from Kaş take visitors on day excursions to the island.

Mooring
Stern-to in the extreme S corner of the harbour, but note that the rather stony bottom provides only moderate holding. Shelter is good, being open only to the NE, although some swell from a north wind would enter.

Facilities

There are tavernas and cafés, and a few shops for provisions, but being Greek they are not open in the afternoon.

A ferry runs occasionally to Rhodes, but you cannot of course use this service if you have not officially entered the country.

KAŞ   36°11′.9N 29°38′.5E   Port of Entry

An agreeable small town, with a reasonably good harbour which is frequently inclined to be rather too lumpy for small yachts.

Mooring
Stern-to the yacht quay on the W side of the harbour. This can become rather congested if one of the cruising flotillas that operate in the area happen to be in port for the night. It may even be necessary to form a second row at the quay.

In moderate to strong W winds, or in S winds, a swell enters the harbour and it can become uncomfortable.

Facilities

⚓ 🛢 ❄ £ ✉ ➘ ⌐ ✎ ⚒ ✚ plus officials for a Port of Entry

Fuel can be collected by canister from a service station just up the road. Water is from a hose on the quay, and small boys will probably offer to collect ice for you from a nearby fishermen's supplier. Turkish gas bottles can be exchanged, and one may even sometimes find Camping gas.

Buses stop here on the route from Fethiye to Antalya.

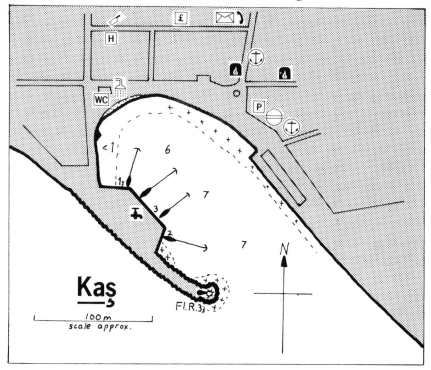

Kaş

FI.R.3s

100 m
scale approx.

KAŞ, South bay   36°10′.5N 29°38′.9E   (No plan)

For a more peaceful mooring, or if Kaş harbour becomes uncomfortable in S or W winds, this very pleasant anchorage lies just over a mile to the SE of the harbour.

The wide bay is divided into two parts by a rocky promontory extending out from its S shore with a conspicuous white house standing on its tip. Anchor either side of this promontory, letting go the anchor in 10 m or more; the sea-bed in both parts in fairly steep-shelving. The bottom is sand and weed. Shelter is quite good in most conditions, but particularly so in S winds.

Looking up at the E shore from the anchorage, a few quite well-preserved ancient rock tombs can be seen, carved into the rock some way up a seemingly inaccessible sheer cliff face.

CHAPTER 29

Kas to Gulf of Antalya

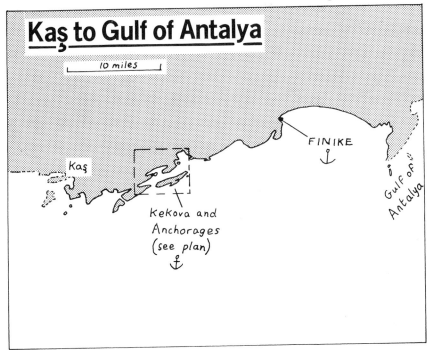

Harbours and anchorages

	Open to:	Comments:
Kekova and Anchorages		
Tersane	NW/N/NE	–
Karaloz	–	Entrance not recommended in strong SE winds
Siçak	NE	–
Siçak, north bay	S/SE/E	–
Üçağiz	–	Choice of anchorages covering any wind direction
Kale	SW/S/SE/E	Only $\frac{1}{2}$ mile fetch to SE to Kekova island
Gökkaya Limani	–	Choice of anchorages depending on wind direction
Finike (harbour)	NE	Swell can enter in east winds

Note: Entering the stretch of water inside Kekova island through the gap at the W end of the island, pass either side of the two islets in the gap, and keep to the centre of the channel in either case. Do not try to pass between these two islets.

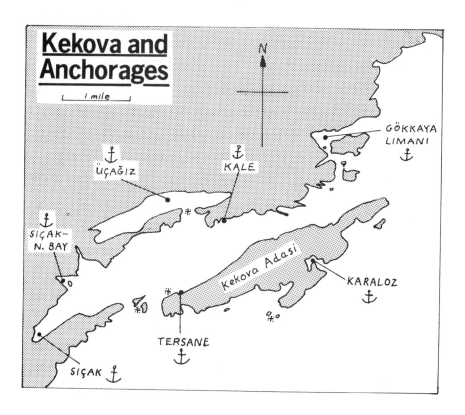

TERSANE   36°10′.3N 29°50′.8E   (No plan)

This small cove on the N coast almost at the W tip of Kekova island, has many interesting ruins both on the beach at the head of the cove, at the water's edge on the W side (although these have been scarred with graffiti), and behind the beach over towards the S coast of the island.

There is no habitation, and the anchorage is delightful except when motorboats arrive with trippers. Unfortunately it is not terribly well sheltered and yachts do not often stay here overnight except in settled weather.

Tersane Bay, Kekova

A small yacht can anchor inside the cove with a stern line to a rock on either shore. Larger yachts will find the cove too small and will have to drop anchor at the mouth, again with a stern line to a rock. The bottom is sand, and depths inside the cove are 4–6 m, but shelving away steeply at the mouth requiring the anchor to be let go there in 15 m or more. Open from W round to NE across to the mainland shore, a fetch of 1 to 1½ miles.

Caution: Between Tersane cove and the western tip of Kekova island keep well clear of the underwater rocks with only 3 m depth, lying about 150 m off the shore of the island.

Also beware of the rocks awash about 150 m SW of the islet Karaadalar, 1½ miles E of the W tip of Kekova island.

KARALOZ   36°11′N 29°53.4′E

A remarkably concealed anchorage in a tiny rocky inlet on the S coast of Kekova island, 1½ miles from its E tip. Just inside the mouth, the inlet

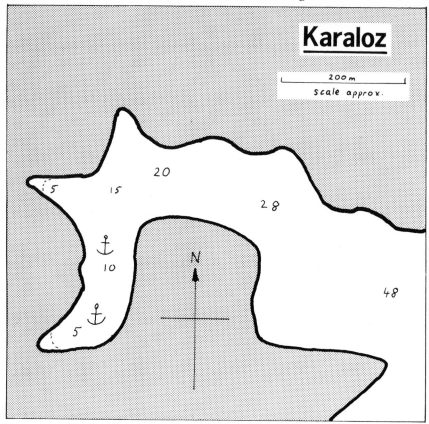

bends tight round to the left, revealing an anchorage large enough for maybe five or six yachts. It is too narrow to swing, and a stern line is essential, but some of the rocks to which to secure a line are very sharp and a loop of chain is advisable. It is even narrow enough at the head to put lines out to both sides and perhaps dispense with the anchor altogether. The bottom is sand and weed.

The entrance is open to the SE and it is not recommended to use the anchorage in strong SE winds. With a big swell from the SE, negotiating the entrance would be difficult, if not impossible.

SIÇAK   36°10′N 29°48′.3E   (No plan)

Well sheltered from the predominant summer W winds, this is a pleasant secluded anchorage at the far W end of the enclosed area of water inside Kekova island, but open to ENE up the sound. There is a large area to anchor and swing, on a steadily shelving muddy bottom, in depths of 4–15 m.

Walking from here in a WSW'ly direction for about ½ mile one comes to the narrow head of Assar bay. Here can be seen the remains of an ancient city reaching right down to the water's edge, and further examination with mask and snorkel reveals that the remains continue into the sea, with what appears to be a road and some walls now underwater.

SIÇAK, North bay 36°10'.6N 29°49'.1E (No plan)

One mile from the Siçak anchorage described above, on the north shore, is this V-shaped bay with a rock and a tiny islet on the left side of the mouth. Enter to the E of this islet, and anchor in 10–14 m on sand, with a stern line to either shore as there is insufficient room to swing. A secluded and quite well-protected spot, open only to E and SE for a short fetch across towards the Tersane anchorage.

ÜÇAĞIZ 36°10'.7N 29°60'.9E

The very small village of Üçağiz lies opposite the entrance to this almost completely enclosed lagoon which is some 1½ miles long, and 400–500 m

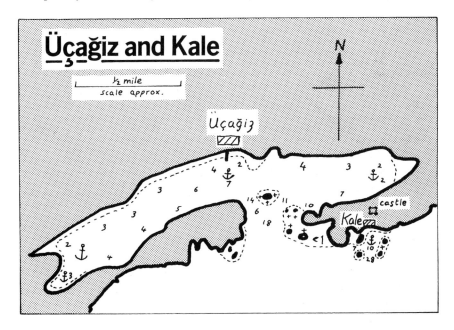

wide. As shown on the plan there are convenient anchoring depths on a muddy bottom over the whole area, so according to conditions one can anchor in complete safety either just off the village, or at the extreme E or W end.

Entering the lagoon keep well clear of the very rocky area on the right hand side of the entrance, and pass either side of the small islet that stands just left of mid-channel, but keep well clear of this islet as it too is surrounded by rocks beneath the surface.

KALE (Castle Bay)   36°10′.4N 29°51′.7E

A difficult anchorage, but in a superb setting beneath the castle just east of the entrance to Üçağiz, with some very picturesque small houses, a few rustic restaurants, and the remains and relics of ancient civilisations scattered around all over the hillside.

Approach the anchorage from practically due south to avoid the rocks, both visible and underwater, on both sides.

The bottom is sand but quite rocky in parts, so it may be difficult to get the anchor to set securely. Once a good hold is achieved, one could run out a stern line either to one of the rocks to the west, or to one of the jetties in front of the restaurants. Depths are 6–15 m.

Kale, Kekova

Shelter is only fair, and if a chop builds up in the channel between Kekova island and the mainland shore, or if a heavy swell is coming in from the W through the gap at the W end of Kekova island, the anchorage will become uncomfortable.

GÖKKAYA LIMANI   36°12'.6N 29°53'.7E

Lying 1 mile NW of the E tip of Kekova island, this bay provides several good spots for anchoring, depending on conditions, protected by the small islet Aşirli Adasi.

Entrance to the bay through the channel north of Aşirli Adasi is free of obstructions. In the channel S of it are a number of rocks above water with others underwater around them, as indicated on the plan.

Protection from W and N is good anywhere in the bay, but some parts are clearly better than others if there is a swell rolling in from the SE or E. Care should be taken in selecting a position to anchor, becaue manoeuvring to re-anchor at night, due to a change in the weather, would be made difficult by the many rocks.

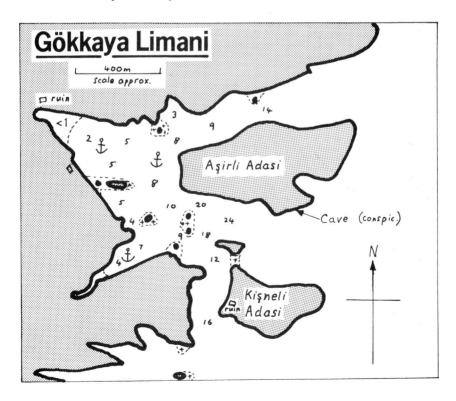

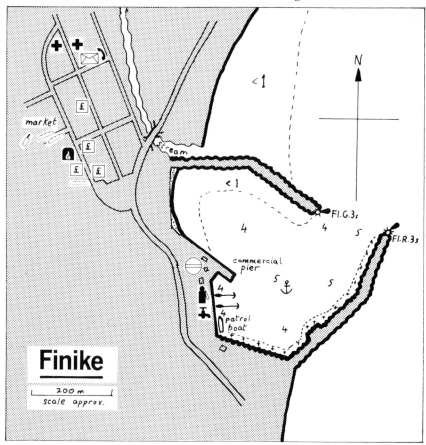

FINIKE   36°17'.7N 30°09'E

This is a large and busy but rather unattractive town, with a safe harbour providing a useful shelter on this stretch of coast. Finike is no longer a Port of Entry, although some guide books still list it as such. Mooring fees are charged in the season.

Mooring
Stern-to on the W wall in ample depths, just S of the commercial pier. The S part of this wall is reserved for the customs patrol boat, and is marked accordingly.

   If a swell from the E makes conditions on the quay troublesome, there is enough room to anchor and swing in the harbour.

Facilities

Fuel and water are on the quay, ice is available, and Turkish gas bottles can be exchanged in town.

Buses stop here on the route from Fethiye to Antalya.

CHAPTER 30

Gulf of Antalya (Antalya Körfezi)

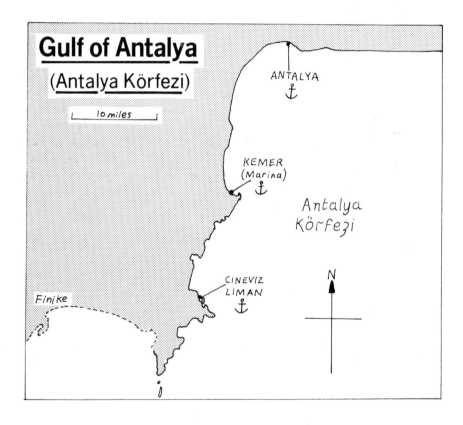

Harbours and anchorages

	Open to:	Comments:
Cineviz Liman	N	Can be uncomfortable in swell from NE
Kemer (marina)	–	–
Antalya (harbour)	SW	All-round protection in small part of the harbour

CINEVIZ LIMAN   36°22'N 30°30'E   (No plan)

An isolated, well sheltered anchorage, 15 miles S of Kemer, and 12 miles NNE of Taşlik Burnu, the cape that marks the SW extreme of the Antalya Gulf.

The bay is entered from the N, and a crop of rocks stand above water in the centre of the mouth, but with deep water on either side. Steep hills rise up from the W shore of the bay to over 1500 ft, and very occasionally strong gusts can sweep down from these hills into the anchorage. However, it is normally safe and peaceful in the summer, well protected from the predominant summer winds that blow either up the gulf from the S, or light to moderate from the NE.

Anchor off the beach at the head of the bay in depths of 4–12 m on soft sand with some weed. It may be advisable to run out a stern line to hold the bows pointing at the mouth, towards any swell that can work in, even though the wind in the enclosed bay might be only light and variable.

Sazak Liman, the bay less than a mile down the coast to the S of Cineviz, is a rather poor anchorage even though it looks quite well protected on the chart. It is open to the E and NE, and even in the predominantly S'ly summer winds some swell will work into the bay, and it is seldom a comfortable anchorage.

KEMER – Marina   36°36'.1N 30°34'.4E

In 1984 all the walls, piers and dredging of this brand new marina were completed, but the buildings for offices, shops, showers, toilets, and so on were still under construction, due to be completed some time in 1985. Until then, the only shops are in the village 15 minutes walk away.

Within two years, this ramshackle village is to be transformed into a major holiday resort, under a government plan to make it a central point from which to encourage the spread of tourism in the surrounding area. Hotels and apartment blocks are being built, and a few are already completed.

Approach and mooring
The marina lies immediately on the W side of the rocky promontory Küçükburun. A wide bay with a Club Mediterranée complex on the shore is on the E side of the promontory.

When approaching from the N, there is a dangerous shoal less than a mile due N of the marina entrance. In 1984 concrete blocks had been

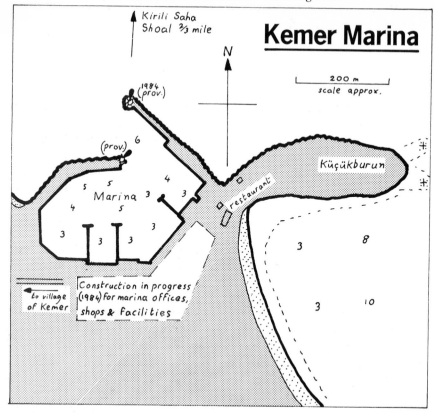

placed on the shoal with the intention of installing a light in the not-too-distant future. The shoal, named on the chart as Kirili Saha, is some 300 m across. As long as one stays a good distance off, it is perfectly safe to pass between it and the shore to the W, although the depths as you approach the marina from this side will be only 6–10 m.

There will eventually be ground tackle with individual bow strops for mooring, as in Kuş Adasi and Bodrum, but until they are installed one can moor either stern-to or alongside on the walls or the piers.

Facilities

The water points around the marina should be operational early in 1985. Fuel and electricity will take a little longer.

Gas bottles, post office, telephones, baker, and grocery shops are in the village, although these will all, in time, be provided in the marina.

It also seems likely that when the marina is fully operational, Kemer will be made a Port of Entry.

ANTALYA   36°53'.1N 30°42'.1E   Port of Entry

Although the modern extensive city of Antalya is the fourth largest in Turkey, from the tiny harbour, enclosed by rocky cliffs, the impression is very different. Many of the old buildings on the harbour front have been tastefully renovated to provide restaurants, cafés, shops, and a quality hotel, all under a government plan to attract holidaymakers and cruising yachts to the town. This showpiece mini-village created around the

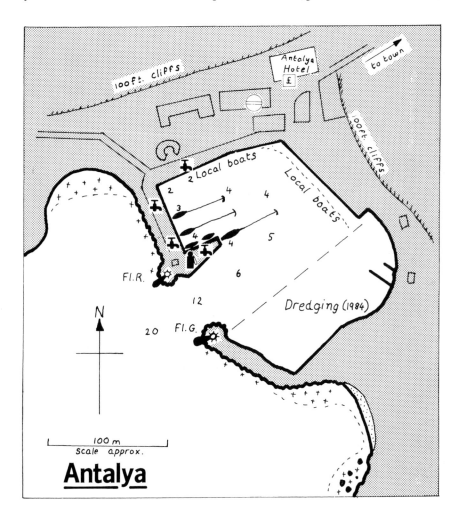

Antalya

harbour has been very well received, not least by the local residents, particularly the younger generation, for whom it seems to have become the fashionable evening meeting place.

At the present, there is only a small area of the harbour for yachts, most of the quay being given over to the boats of local fishermen, who hold a sometimes quite noisy market every day soon after sunrise to dispose of their catch. However, as part of the development plan it seems the fishing boats will in due course be moved out to make more space for yachts, but exactly where they will be moved to, nobody seems quite sure, the only other nearby shelter being the new shipping port 5 miles down the coast.

Visiting yachts often stay for several days in Antalya, whilst their crews take to the road by bus or hire-car to tour the many places of interest in the area round about. These are so numerous it is impossible to describe them all here. The most interesting are the extensive ruins of a major city at Side, dating from several centuries BC, as well as other archeological sites at Perge and Aspendos; waterfalls at Düden and Manavgat; and the breathtaking natural rock formations at Göreme with cave-like dwellings carved into the soft volcanic rock together with two complete towns, one large enough for an estimated 2000 people, excavated underground to a depth of eight storeys.

Approach and mooring

When approaching Antalya from the S the modern buildings of the town are clearly seen spread along the cliff-top about 100 ft above the sea level. The harbour lies approximately in the centre of the built-up area, just to the right of the tallest building on the skyline.

Close inshore, about 400 m W of the harbour entrance is a black buoy marking a wreck. The entrance itself is quite narrow, and open to the SW. In a heavy swell from the S or SE, entering the harbour can be very difficult, particularly for larger yachts. Manoeuvring room inside is very restricted, and the sheltered area reserved for yachts, around to the left side, is tiny. In summer it often becomes congested, and yachts moor two or three abreast from the quay, which means that several become well boxed in.

Efforts are being made to provide more space for yachts, including the dredging out of the SE side of the harbour, and the construction here of a concrete pontoon. But unfortunately, unless further extensions are made to the breakwaters (and this doesn't seem likely in the immediate future) the new pontoon will inevitably be prone to some swell in the predominant S/SE'ly winds of summer afternoons and evenings.

In the existing space for yachts, protection from the S is good. The surge is only disturbing in very strong S winds which in summer are unlikely to occur, except perhaps at the beginning and end of the season.

Facilities

🕯 ⚓ 🔥 ❄ £ ✉ ⌇ ⌇ / ✎ 🔲 ✚ D

plus officials for a Port of Entry

The customs office is on the harbour front, but unfortunately the health, harbour master and passport offices are 5 miles away in the shipping port.

Fuel and water are right on the quay, and there is usually someone offering to collect ice for you. Gas bottles, but only of the Turkish variety, can be exchanged in town. Other bottles can be refilled if deposited for 24 hours.

There are restaurants and cafés around the harbour, but their prices are considerably higher than in the town. Also in the town are a much greater variety of provisions than are stocked by the small supermarket beside the harbour.

There are a few electricity points on the quay.

The large bus station serves all parts of Turkey, and the nearby airport has domestic services as well as a few charters and other international flights to and from Europe.

APPENDICES

APPENDIX 1

Glossary of Useful Words – Greek and Turkish

	Turkish	*Greek* (phonetic)
water	su	nero
diesel	mazot	petreleo
petrol	benzin	venzeeni
bottled gas	tüpgaz	petrogaz
cooking alcohol	gaz	petrogaz petreleo
grease	gres	grasso
oil	yağ	laadi
yacht	yat	cottero
GRP	polyester	polyestair
wood	tahta	xilo
steel	saç	sidero
stainless steel	paslanmaz celik	anoxidato
aluminium	aliminyum	aluminio
galvanised	galvaniz	galvanisé
brass	bakir	broonzo
screws	vida	veedez
nuts	somun	paximaria
bolts	saplama	bolonia
machine screws	vida baş	frezatez
anchor	çapa	ankira
chain	zincir	alisida
rope	halat	skini
propeller	pervane	propeller
battery	batarya	battaria
electric wire	tel elektrik	kalothia
flag	bayrak	simiya
chart	harita	harti

	Turkish	*Greek* (phonetic)
engineer/mechanic	mekanik	mekanicos
electrician	elekçi	electrologos
wind	ruzgar	aiyera
swell	dalga	thalassa
harbour	liman	limani
ship's papers	tekne kağat	hartia
passport	pasaport	deeyavetirio
passport office	pasaport merkezi	ipiresia alothapon
customs	gümrük	teleneo
health office	sihiye	–
harbour master's office/port captain	liman	limenarkio
yes	evet	nay
no	hayir	okhi
help!	yardim	voithia
forwards	ileri	brosta
backwards	geri	peeso
haul in	çek	vira
slacken off	koyver	laska

Greek Chart Abbreviations – Light Characteristics

British	Greek	British	Greek
F	Στ.	Mo	Mo.
Oc	Δλ. or Δσμ.Δλ.	Al	Εν.
Iso	Ισο.		
Fl	'Αν or Δσμ.'Αν	W	Λ
LFl	–	R	Εϱ
Q	Σπθ	G	Πϱ
IQ	Σπθ. Διαϰ	Y	Κτ/Ποϱτ
VQ	–	Bu	Κ
IVQ	–	Vi	'Ιόϰ
UQ	–	s	δ
IUQ	–		

Turkish charts use the old form of British abbreviations as used on British Admiralty fathoms charts.

Index

Note: Page references in italics refer to plans.